MW00680271

# COLLECTING ROMANCE NOVELS

## DAWN E. RENO AND JACQUE TIEGS

*Alliance Publishers*

ISBN 0-9641509-5-6

Cover and Interior Design by Cynthia Dunne
Produced by Publisher's Studio, Albany, New York

Alliance Books are available
at special discounts for bulk purchases
for sales and promotions, premiums, fund
raising, or educational use.
For details, contact:

Alliance Publishing, Inc.
P.O. Box 080377
Brooklyn, New York 11208-0002

Distributed to the trade by National Book Network, Inc.

10 8 6 4 2 1 3 5 7 9

John Ennis, a leader in romance book cover art,
has kindly provided the authors with
permission to feature his cover art for
*Circle of Light* (author: Nancy Cane) on the
cover of this volume. Ennis has created
hundreds of covers for all the
major paperback romance publishers.

# ACKNOWLEDGEMENTS

We'd like to thank Kathryn Falk and the *Romantic Times* convention staff for bringing us together. If we hadn't met each other in Nashville, we would never have done this book.

To the editors of *Essence of Romance* (Twilight Publishing), our gratitude for sharing valuable information.

To the romance authors, our heartfelt thanks for your support and for the wonderful stories you've all created.

Special thanks to our photographer, Robert Reno, who offered his time and energy to photograph all the books illustrated herein.

Also, much of the tremendous support and backing we've received has come from our editor, Dorothy Harris, a wonderfully strong woman with a good sense of humor and sound business acumen. May you have nothing but happy days and much success!

# CONTENTS

# INTRODUCTION

At a recent romance writers' and readers' convention, Jacque and I were drawn together by a mutual interest: collecting. Jacque had given a workshop on collecting romance novels and I had already written half a dozen books on collecting antiques and art. We both agreed the time was right for a book which would help romance readers and collectors identify and price the books they loved best. Our editor, Dottie Harris, agreed wholeheartedly with us. But, where to start?

After long hours of discussion, we narrowed down our focus to books written from the 1970s to the present. These are the novels for which most collectors are searching. We also realized that there are probably many readers who have no idea how to find their favorite authors' books. We hope this volume will provide readers and collectors with resources other than their libraries so they can join our circle of romance enthusiasts.

We also decided that we would only cover traditional romance novels in this volume and that we would address the fascinating topics of autographed books, bookmarks, posters, and other collectibles in a future book. We also encourage readers to contact us to let us know about other resources they're finding useful in expanding their collections and to tell us what areas in the field they'd like to see us cover in the future.

*Happy reading and collecting!*

DAWN E. RENO AND JACQUE TIEGS

# HOW TO BE AN INSTANT EXPERT IN ROMANCE NOVEL COLLECTING

## CHAPTER 1

## WHAT YOU NEED TO KNOW ABOUT COLLECTING ROMANCE NOVELS

Although romances have been around since the Brontë sisters began writing them in the mid–1800s, it wasn't until the late 1960s–early 1970s that they became wildly popular. The romance novel is, therefore, a recent phenomenon in the book publishing industry. The genre has grown by leaps and bounds and now boasts a 50 percent market share of today's fiction. Yes, romances make up nearly half of all the novels sold in the world!

There are many different types of romance novels and hundreds (perhaps thousands) of authors toward whom readers gravitate. However, most of the ones considered collectible are those which are considered "category books."

Category books are published by such monster companies as Harlequin and Silhouette. Every four to six weeks, each line introduces three to six new books. Most of the category romances are published in small quantities and have a very short "shelf life." In booksellers' terms, "shelf life" means the amount of time a particular book will take up space in the bookstore. Because category romances are published on such a regular basis, the old ones are cleaned off the shelves to make room for the new month's selections. Thus, a category romance book will have a shelf life of approximately six weeks. Once the book is off the shelf, the only places a reader or fan is likely to find it will be in a used bookstore, a thrift store, or at a garage sale.

Some companies offer their readers a subscription service, which means the reader gets that month's offerings at the same time (or earlier) than the bookstore receives its copies. Each book/author is given the same weight when a publisher prints for a subscription service. As a result, a popular author's print run will be the same as that of a new author since both books are going out in the same monthly subscription package.

Publishers almost never do reprints of category books. Thus, once the book is off the shelf, it is not likely the reader will see it again. However, when an author achieves a certain degree of popularity, it is often in a publisher's best interest to republish the author's earlier works. This has been the case with such prolific authors as Nora Roberts, Barbara Delinsky, and Janet Dailey. When these writers reached the heights of the bestseller list, their once small press run category romances were re-packaged, new covers were designed, and they were brought out once again—but this time, as "big books." The publishers allowed reprints, bigger press runs, and, as a result, the books had longer shelf lives.

Bookstore clerks (especially in small or used bookstores) help to boost an author's popularity by recommending personal favorites to their readers. If a reader happens to fall in love with one particular author's style, more than likely she or he will search the bookstores for other books that author wrote. If the author is writing series romances, it will be difficult to find old titles at a regular bookstore, so the reader will have to turn to other resources such as yard and garage sales, flea markets and bazaars. If the author becomes famous enough, those old, original category romances automatically become more valuable.

Thus, the major ingredient that makes a romance book collectible is its author. Perhaps an author or a specific book received a glowing review in a publication such as *Romantic Times* (a magazine devoted to romances, their authors and their fans) or in a local or national newspaper. Once a book or an author receives positive publicity, sales improve rapidly. This is the catalyst which makes the author's books more valuable to the collector.

At that point, the book searcher's job begins. Once a customer expresses interest in a certain author, the bookstore's research person (the searcher) will start hunting down copies of the author's books by word of mouth, long distance phone calls, faxes, and on-line searches. In 1993, when bookstores realized there were many collectors who were searching for works by specific romance authors, the stores joined together and formed the Great American Booksearch Network. (Members are listed in Chapter 4.) By talking with each other, searchers and the bookstores they worked for understood which authors were in demand; little by little, it became obvious that there was a trend, a silent undercurrent in the publishing business. Those romance books that husbands all over the world dreamed of dumping into the trash were suddenly becoming valued collectibles!

## ESSENTIALS ON COLLECTING ROMANCE NOVELS

In addition to knowing that these books have small print runs and short shelf lives, the collector should know how to tell the age of a book and whether or not it is a first edition, book club edition, or subscription edition.

There are two ways to check whether a book is a first edition:

(1) Look at the copyright date which is always listed on the reverse of the title page. It should be the same as the print date. Also, at the bottom of the copyright page, you will see a line of numbers which usually starts at 10 and runs down to 1. If the book is a first edition, all ten numbers will be listed; if it is a second edition, the 1 will be missing; if it is a third, the 2 will be missing, and so on.

(2) Check the cover art date. If it is a reprint, there will be two dates instead of one. WARNING: Recently, it has been noted that some cover art has been used for more than one book. Therefore, two totally different books have had the same cover. Although most publishers make every effort to ensure that this does not happen, there are some books which have slipped through—and, as a result, have become more valuable to the collector.

In addition to checking the above information, also remember that for various reasons some authors write under more than one name. In Chapter 2, we include a list of authors and their pseudonyms to enable you to successfully complete your collection. So you can cover every available avenue in your search, we've also included information about different mail order subscription lists run by book distributors and publishers, computer services for romance readers and collectors and newsletters and magazines which cover this industry.

We have also provided a Key Words section for our readers. Even if you are a novice in romance collecting, the Key Words section will help you become an educated consumer, quickly and efficiently.

## KEY WORDS TO
## KNOW TO COLLECT ROMANCE NOVELS

1. Category—romances published in small quantities, with short "shelf lives"; most collectible books on the market.

2. Edition—the original publication of a book and each reissue in which it is substantially revised; reissues in different form, e.g., paperback, illustrated, where there are no substantial revisions in substance.

3. Time travel—a type of romance in which one of the main characters travels backward or forward in time to find romance.

4. Condition—the state in which a book is found, e.g., pristine, used by book collectors to describe a paperback which is in perfect or mint condition.

5. Genre—the type of book; indicates subject or theme, e.g., mystery, romance, historical, science fiction.

6. Historical—a romance novel set in a time period usually 100 years or more before the present.

7. Contemporary—a romance story set in the present.

8. Erotica—that form of writing which leans toward sexuality or sensuality.

9. Big books—usually of contemporary genre, of general interest, typically lengthy and sold widely throughout the market with large press runs.

10. Small books—usually short books with smaller press runs.

11. Shelf life—amount of time a book will take up space in a bookstore.

12. Imprint—a series or type of book produced by a publisher, e.g., Harlequin Intrigue, Candlelight Ecstasy, Silhouette Shadows; also called "lines" by readers and collectors.

13. Young Adult—published for teenagers, with plots and characters relevant to that book reading population, e.g., the Wildfire imprint.

# A BRIEF HISTORY OF ROMANCE NOVELS

## CHAPTER 2

The *Random House Dictionary* defines romance as "a story that tells of heroic deeds, adventure, and love; to indulge in fanciful stories; a love affair; an appealing or romantic quality." The *Doubleday Dictionary* calls romance "adventurous, fascinating, of picturesque nature or appeal; the romance of faraway places; disposition to delight in the mysterious, adventurous, sentimental, etc.; a love affair; a long narrative from medieval legend, involving heroes in strange adventures and affairs of love; any fictitious narrative embodying adventure, love affairs, etc.; the class of literature consisting of romances; an extravagant falsehood."

Anyone who has read and loved a romance can tell you they embody all these definitions and more. Romances constitute almost 50 percent of today's fiction sales—which is quite a chunk of the market! Romance fans are the most loyal readers alive. They anxiously await the newest books from their favorite authors or another in the line of romances they prefer to read. Some booksellers have estimated that romance readers spend an average of $200 per month on romantic novels; thus, it is not surprising that some of these novels are now collectors' favorites.

Although this book deals only with romances written from 1970 to the present, the history of the romance is an old and well-known genre.

Marie de France, a late twelfth-century French poet, was the first female recognized as writing what both the *Doubleday* and *Random House* dictionaries describe as "romance." Her writings, known as *lais* are short story-poems based on Breton tales in which the love relationship is clearly defined, as is the adventurous nature of its participants. The stories involve sympathetic characters in fairy-tale-like settings. Each hero is noble, brave and passionately in love with the heroine. No matter whether the story ends tragically, as so many of the early romances did, or happily-ever-after, the two lovers fight against family, nation, and nature's elements to come together, setting the stage for the romance style which blossomed many centuries later.

It wasn't until the Brontë sisters—Anne, Charlotte and Emily—began penning romantic tales at their kitchen table that the guidelines for future romance writers were created. The Brontë sisters were products of a society in which women were not permitted to publish; in fact, Charlotte Brontë's *Jane Eyre* was originally published under the male pseudonym Currer Bell in October, 1847. Although *Jane Eyre* attracted a great deal of attention from the literary community, Charlotte felt that her "passport to a society of clever people . . . was of no use."

Emily Brontë's *Wuthering Heights* received unenthusiastic reviews when it was published under the pseudonym of Ellis Bell in 1847. A second edition was published in 1850, in which Charlotte did considerable editing of the work. Anne, the third Brontë sister to write, was the author of *Agnes Grey*, a lesser recognized work.

Charlotte Brontë admitted to a "passionate preference for the wild, wonderful, and thrilling."

She wrote *Jane Eyre* against her principles, forced to do so by commercial necessity. Yet, there are many times in that book (and in an earlier work, *The Professor* which was not published until after *Jane Eyre*) where Brontë lets down her guard and permits the reader to see how she, a strong woman who might be considered a feminist, feels.

The first romances were women's explorations of the home and the hearth, and the surrounding environs. It was strange to find the heroine of *Jane Eyre* travelling alone, although it is commonplace in most of today's romances. The Brontë sisters followed their hearts when they wrote about the society they knew, the romances they dreamed, and the men for whom they longed. Little did they realize the genre they developed would be emulated for centuries to come.

Literary women, such as Harriet Beecher Stowe, Christina Rossetti, Charlotte Brontë, George Sand, Jane Austen, Emily Dickinson, Elizabeth Barrett Browning, and George Eliot were credited by their critics and literary experts as having "romantic fervor and depths of soul." These are not terms generally used for male writers. Each of these women penned a work we would term "romantic," using the dictionary definition. Each of the classic romances was written by a woman who may never have had a "room of her own," using Virginia Woolf's terminology, but those authors who made money at their craft all wrote about the subjects they knew much better than did their male counterparts—romance, marriage, and family.

In the 1920s, romance took a turn for the sexier with D. H. Lawrence's books, *Lady Chatterley's Lover*, *Sons and Lovers* and *Women in Love*. Lawrence's broader strokes of romantic sensuality shocked the world and the books were often banned. As a result, many different versions of *Lady Chatterley's Lover*, for instance, have been published.

Women began writing romance serials for newspapers in Europe and America in the 1920s and continued through the 1940s, but the works never received recognition in the literary world as did the Brontë sisters' books. In fact, it is even difficult to identify these women writers today.

Finally, Margaret Mitchell introduced a romance called *Gone With the Wind*, during a period when the world was upset by war and threats of war. It was a book that captured the hearts and minds of women across the United States. The heroine, Scarlett O'Hara, was an independent, feisty woman with her own mind. At first, Scarlett could be considered conceited and selfish. But as the story of her life and her romances with Rhett Butler and Ashley Wilkes unfolded, Scarlett developed into a great character, finding the strength which enabled her to live through the horrors of the Civil War and through more tragedies than anyone should have to endure.

Modern romance writers have, for the most part, followed the traditional romance formula: boy meets girl (or vice versa); they have an immediate attraction but are separated by their own personalities or other impediments; then—somewhere near the end of the book—they recognize the depth of their love for one another and overcome all the obstacles in their path. Of course, in the happy ending, boy and girl are together.

There are, however, dramatic differences between the traditional romance and the modern formula. The majority of today's romances feature strong, independent female leads who are on the same level as, or above, their male counterparts, in career or financial position. The endings don't all focus on marriage, but the couple does confess their love, sometimes makes love, or may live with each other.

Although the literary world seems to denigrate romance books, readers fight for their right to read them, perhaps seeking to escape from what has become a world fraught with danger and sadness to a place where love, tenderness and empathy envelop the reader.

Granted, most modern romances can't approach the timeless appeal of Catherine's and Heathcliff's enduring love in *Wuthering Heights* or Scarlett and Rhett's steamy unions in *Gone With the Wind*. But no one ever imagined that the works of Shakespeare or Dickens would outlive their authors. Suffice it to say, the romance novel you're reading at this moment could be one of the classics of the future.

## KEY ELEMENTS
## THAT DISTINGUISH ROMANCES

The categories of romance are as varied as the stories themselves. Some are serials or small, short books with strict guidelines; others are sagas which span more than one generation. There are mainstream romances which are typically concerned with contemporary times, characters who are glitzy or wealthy, and settings which are glamorous or fascinating. Western romances are where the cowboy keeps his hat on and the woman at his side is capable and strong; Native American tales are where one or both of the main characters are tribal members; science fiction romances are set on other planets; gay romances stretch the romantic limits, always looking for different slants on a same sex story; feminist romances involve plots which do not necessarily culminate in marriage and a happily-ever-after ending, but, instead, are concerned with the needs of today's strong heroines. And then there are time travel stories, a fairly new addition to the genre and one to which some die-hard romance fans are gravitating in droves. Historicals are popular with readers who are curious about other times or places. The readers of Regencies are quite astute about the Regency period and enjoy these light, humorous tales; suspenseful or intriguing romance tales involve plots which keep readers turning the pages; ethnic romances, a recent arrival on the romance market, have African-American, Asian-American or Hispanic-American characters and are geared for those ethnic readers in the romance market; gothics, like those originally created by the Brontë sisters, still enjoy an active readership, as do Edwardians. And, the latest to titillate readers, the fantasy of having a vampire, ghost or werewolf as a lover!

For more information about each series and what they represent, please see the section entitled "Major Publishers" later in this chapter.

### MAJOR PUBLISHERS AND
### THEIR ROMANCE IMPRINTS

As a note, there are novels which are included in the price guide section of this book which are

*Diana Palmer's* Love on Trial *(An Original MacFadden Romance, #218).* Courtesy of Jacque Tiegs.

published by companies not listed here. Some of these publishers have gone out of business, which makes their books more rare and, thus, more collectible. For example, the MacFadden romances are in great demand because they are no longer in print. Their Encore line was written by such authors as Diana Palmer, Jayne Bentley and Jayne Castle.

Other romance publishers which are now out of business include Beagle, Gallen, Major, Mystique, Tapestries, To Have and To Hold, Avon's Scarlett Ribbons series, Avon Ribbons, Second Chance, and Coventry. Gallen published some of the original historicals and contemporary books. Second Chance books were published by Berkley in the late 1980s (authors include Steffie Hall, Kay Hooper, and Sandra Brown), while Candlelight Ecstasy Supremes

*Anne Stuart's*
Barrett's Hill *(Beagle).*
*Courtesy of Jacque Tiegs.*

*Diana Stuart's* Cry for
Paradise *(Gallen
Historical Romance).*
*Courtesy of Jacque Tiegs.*

*Liliane Robin's*
Fury on the Pampas
*(Mystique Books, #86).*
*Courtesy of Jacque Tiegs.*

*Cally Hughes'* Treasure
to Share *(Second Chance
at Love/To Have and to
Hold, #25).*
*Courtesy of Jacque Tiegs.*

*Patricia Veryan's*
Love's Duet
*(Coventry Romances).*
*Courtesy of Jacque Tiegs.*

were published by Dell in the 1980s (authors include Bonnie Drake, Lori Copeland, Diana Blayne, Jackie Black, Amii Lorin and Heather Graham). Dell also published Candlelight Regencies by authors like Kay Hooper; and Candlelight Ecstasy by such authors as Jayne Castle, Lori Copeland, Heather Graham, Cathy Linz and Amii Lorin.

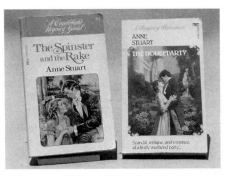

*Two of Anne Stuart's Regencies:* The Spinster and the Rake *(Candlelight Regency Special, #711) and* The Houseparty *(Fawcett).* Courtesy of Jacque Tiegs.

Avalon Books publishes wholesome romances for both teenagers and adults. These short (175-200 page) books are contemporary romances, mysteries or historical westerns which involve heroines who have interesting careers or professions.

Avon Books publishes writers from almost every type of romance genre, including contemporaries, historicals, science fiction, fantasy, regencies, suspense, mysteries and westerns. Most of the books are larger-size novels, ranging from 350-500 pages. Authors include Catherine Hart, Ana Leigh, Connie Brockway, Loretta Chase, Glenda Sanders, and Kathleen Woodiwiss.

Ballantine/Fawcett/Ivy Books publishes single title Regencies, historicals and contemporaries. Authors include Jeanne Carmichael, Susan Carroll, Joan Smith, and Kristin Hannah.

Bantam Doubleday Dell's popular Loveswept series of romances focuses on contemporary stories which are approximately 225 pages long and feature great dialogue rather than long narratives. Romance is the focus of the story at all times, although other elements may be intertwined in the hero and heroine's relationship. Bantam also does mainstream/commercial women's fiction of approximately 400-600 pages in length. Authors include Amanda Quick, Ruth Owen, Patricia Potter, Sandra Chastain, Roseanne Bittner, Elizabeth Thornton and many others.

*Cathie Linz's* Winner Takes All (*Candlelight Ecstasy #266*).
*Courtesy of Jacque Tiegs.*

The Berkley Publishing Group imprints include Berkley, Berkley Trade Paperbacks, Jove and Diamond. The group publishes historical, mainstream, mysteries, suspense, Regencies and soft romance titles of all sizes from authors such as Suzanne Forster, Carla Neggers, Catherine Coulter, Nora Roberts, Linda Lael Miller, Katherine Sutcliffe, Jodi Thomas, LaVyrle Spencer, Miriam Minger, Constance O'Day-Flannery, Doris Parmett, Barbara Cartland, Jill Marie Landis and many others.

Branden Publishing Co., Inc. publishes romances with well-drawn characters and stories which reflect the problems of today's society.

Dell Romances/Delacorte are contemporary and historical, sensual and sweet, mysteries and general fiction (including hardcovers). These books are written by such popular authors as Meryl Sawyer, Joan Hohl, Kat Martin, and Virginia Henley.

Dell also publishes the Candlelight line. Some of the Candlelight Ecstasy authors include Jayne Castle, Lori Copeland, Heather Graham, Cathy Linz and Amii Lorin.

Goodfellow Press publishes mainstream romantic fiction, which they call "smooth and seamless." A new company, their guidelines call for novels approximately 85,000 to 125,000 words in length.

Harlequin is one of the first and largest publishers who concentrate on romances. Harlequin adds new imprints to their list all the time. In fact, they are now in the process of preparing a mainstream imprint called "Mira," which is designed to compete with *The New York Times* bestsellers and debuted in 1994. The "Mira" books are not be packaged in the same manner as other Harlequins. They will include intense drama, family sagas, intrigue, and romantic suspense of 400-500 pages written by top romance authors, so be on the lookout for them in your favorite bookstore.

Other Harlequin lines include Harlequin American, an imprint featuring contemporary romances which captures "The Spirit of America." They are fast-paced, action-packed, lively and upbeat American fairy tales which are fairly sensual and usually average 250-300 pages in length. Some of the authors who have written for this series include Anne Stuart, Linda Randall Wisdom, Charlotte Maclay, Dallas Schultze and Jackie Weger.

Harlequin Historical romances are set in the 1700–1900 time period in North America, England or France. Softly sensual, they are often 350-500 pages in length. Some of this imprint's authors include DeLoras Scott, Ruth Langan, Miranda Jarrett, Erin Yorke, Suzanne Barclay and Maura Seger.

Harlequin Intrigue books have plots which focus on a mystery, combining romance with suspense and adventure. The 250-300-page story might range from an everyday event with an odd or ironic twist to whodunits, murder mysteries, psychological suspense books, thrillers, espionage stories, adventures or just plain ol' puzzlers. Authors who write for this series include M. J. Rodgers, Margaret Chittenden,

Rebecca York, Laura Pender and Vickie York.

Harlequin Presents are 200-250-page books written by foreign authors and are set in exotic locales with a sensuous twist. Some of the line's popular authors are Anne Mather, Robyn Donald and Roberta Leigh.

Harlequin Romance novels are shorter (150-200 pages), traditional romances with no explicit sex scenes, emphasizing the emotional rather than the physical aspect of the love affair. The books, appropriate for young adults, are written

*Margaret Chittenden's* This Time Forever *(Harlequin Dreamscape Romance).* Courtesy of Jacque Tiegs.

by such writers as Bethany Campbell, Debbie Macomber, Susan Fox, Anne Marie Duquette and many others.

Harlequin Superromance stories are contemporary, passionate and provocative tales which celebrate life and love and often are quite complex stories with mainstream-type subjects. Their 300-350 page length give writers like Margaret Chittenden, Karen Young, Margot Dalton, Judith Arnold, Sharon Brondos and Marissa Carroll a chance to explore the sensuous side of the romance.

The Harlequin Temptation line is the most sensuous of Harlequin's offerings. These 200-250-page bold, sensuous and often controversial stories are truly innovative. In fact, quite a number of this line's authors such as Jayne Ann Krentz, Barbara Delinsky, Glenda Sanders, Tiffany White and Candace Schuler have gone on to mainstream careers.

HarperCollins publishes several imprints of romances, including paperbacks which are contemporary and historical, women's fiction, romantic suspense, mysteries and thrillers. Some of Harper's authors include Terry Lynn, Millie Criswell,

*Anne Mather's* Devil in Velvet *(Mills & Boon).*
Courtesy of Jacque Tiegs.

*Carla Kelly's* Miss Chartley's Guided Tour *(Signet Regency Romance).*
Courtesy of Jacque Tiegs.

Catherine Anderson, Georgette Heyer, Patricia Hagan, Mary Spencer and others.

Leisure Books' line *LoveSpell* was recently developed to publish all romance titles, especially historical romances of 300+ pages, time travel romances of 250-300 pages, and futuristic romances of 250-300 pages. Their authors include Nancy Cane, Shirl Henke, Amii Lorin, Christine Michels, Nelle McFather, Cinnamon Burke, Paris Afton Bonds and Roberta Gellis.

Lionhearted Publishing, Inc. publishes contemporary, fantasy, time travel, historical and Regencies. This is a new firm whose authors include Marilyn Clay.

Mills & Boon, Ltd. publishes single title/romance/glitz, which are all contemporary lines, usually 200-300 pages in length. Authors include Kathleen O'Brien.

Nal/Signet (Penguin) publishes Regency romances. Their *Topaz* series includes steamy romances, historicals and time travel stories with covers graced by model/spokesperson Steve Sandalis. Authors include Patricia Gaffney, Elisabeth Fairchild, Donna Davidson, Margaret Evans Porter, Marjorie Farrell, Sheila Walsh,

Olivia Fontayne, Catherine Coulter and Deborah Martin.

Pocket Books publishes historicals and some mainstream romances written by authors such as Arnette Lamb, Ivana Trump, Charlene Cross and Sue Rich.

Random House publishes women's fiction, romance, westerns, science fiction and mystery.

Silhouette Books, now a division of Harlequin Enterprises, publishes a number of romance series for adults such as:

Silhouette Romances: contemporary adult romances, modern relationships where the hero and heroine don't make love until they are married. Approximately 225-275 pages long, written by such authors as Terri Lindsey, Carla Cassidy, Stephanie James and many others.

Silhouette Special Editions: sophisticated, substantial books of approximately 275-300 pages. Sensuality may be subtle or sizzling, the plot may be innovative or traditional, but most important, they are very special contemporary romances by authors such as Debbie Macomber, Laurie Paige, Lisa Jackson, Stephanie James, Diana Palmer and many others.

*Mary Lynn Baxter's* Shared Moments *(Silhouette Desire, #24).* From the collection of Peg Reno.

*Diana Palmer's* Reluctant Father *(Silhouette Desire, #469).* From the collection of Peg Reno.

Silhouette Desires: novels ranging from 220-275 pages, written for today's woman. The focus is on the developing relationship and lovemaking is never taken lightly. They are written by Anne Marie Winston, Carole Buck, Diana Palmer, Elizabeth Lowell and many other talented writers.

Silhouette Intimate Moments: a more sensual romance series, with longer stories (350-400 pages) and more complex plots. Designed to give the reader the same flash and excitement as a mainstream romance, the Intimate Moments series is comprised of stories which are adventurous, suspenseful, melodramatic and glamorous. Authors include Elizabeth Lowell, Rachel Lee, Nora Roberts, Erin St. Claire and many others.

*Rachel Lee's* Miss Emmaline and the Archangel *(Silhouette Intimate Moments, #482).* Courtesy of Jacque Tiegs.

Silhouette Shadows: contemporary gothic romances, approximately 350-400 pages long, which revolve around shadowy plots concerning the darker side of love.

St. Martin's Press publishes longer historicals and contemporaries and some fantasy and time travel by such well-known authors as Katherine Deauxville, Kate Coscarelli and Jane Bonander.

Starlog Press publishes historical novels under their Rhapsody Romance imprint and contemporary fiction under their Moonlight Romance imprint.

TOR publishes historicals, suspense, fantasy, and mainstream mysteries.

Warner Books had the distinction of publishing *The Bridges of Madison County*, one of the best-selling romances of all time, which has spent over two years on the bestseller's list. They also publish paperback and hardcover women's fiction, contemporary and historical books by such popular authors as Jayne Ann Krentz, Robert James Waller, Rebecca Brandewyne and Karen Robards.

Zebra and Pinnacle books are now publishing hardcover romances under their Kensington imprint, as well as paperbacks. Their Lovegram, Heartfire, Denise Little Presents and To Love Again imprints produce contemporary romances, historicals, mysteries, mainstream stories, suspense, gothic, Regencies and Native American works by such authors as Janelle Taylor, Sandra Kitt, Georgina Gentry, Dawn Reno, Barbara Bickmore, Shannon Drake (Heather Graham), Katherine Stone, Kathleen Drymon, Constance O'Banyon, Lisa Jackson and many others.

## ROMANCE AUTHORS: THEIR PSEUDONYMS AND GENRES

When you begin a collection of any kind, the first thing you must become familiar with is the product—in this case, the types of books written and their publishers. Now that we've discussed romance publishers and their specialties, let's focus on the authors themselves and the publishers for whom they've written. Since the publishing business is a constantly changing one, authors often move from "house" to "house" when their career is heating up. Or they might leave one publisher to follow their editor to another. Whatever the case, writers often work for more than one publisher during their career; thus, if you find that some of the authors listed are now writing for another line or publisher, this is within the normal course of business.

You may also find that your favorite author has written under different names. Authors use pseudonyms for various reasons. They may want to expand out of their typical genre to try something new, while not giving up their original publisher. In this case, they may work with another publishing company and write under an assumed name.

Some authors use pseudonyms simply because their own names are not "romantic-sounding." If an author is male in this typically female-oriented business, a publisher might ask the man to assume a woman's name so he can write romances and attract a female readership. Another reason authors assume pseudonyms is to collaborate on creative works. Also, many publishers like to "own" their writers' names; thus, if a writer works for another publisher, the author must do so using another name.

Sometimes the way authors choose their pseudonyms is quite ingenious. For example, the E. in A. E. Maxwell (Elizabeth Lowell's pseudonym) stands for Evan, which is her husband's name. Sandra Brown chose the pseudonym Rachel Ryan because those were her children's names. Jude Devereaux slipped her family name Montgomery into her books.

Other writers have actively promoted their books by being part of them in some fashion. Danielle Steel has personally introduced the television movies made from her books; the O'Hurley books show author Nora Roberts on the back cover; and Heather Graham and her family actually posed for the cover illustration for her historical *Tomorrow the Glory*. She was the first author whose publisher used this creative promotional concept.

Although we are highlighting authors who are considered contemporary romance writers, since they appear to be those collectors search for, you will find some old favorites in the following list. Perhaps these are the authors whose works you will choose to add to your collection!

We know this list is probably not comprehensive, so if you don't spot your favorite author, please drop us a note c/o Alliance Publishing, 595 Berriman Street, Brooklyn, New York, 11208 and we'll add it to our growing list.

| AUTHOR/pseudonyms | GENRE |
|---|---|

**Abbott, Jane Worth** .............. category
(a.k.a. Stella Cameron and Virginia Myers)

**Adair, Cherry** ................... category
(a.k.a. Cherry Wilkinson)

**Adams, Audra** ................... category
(a.k.a. Marie Tracy)

**Adams, Dorsey** .................. category
(a.k.a. Dorsey Kelley)

**Adams, Joyce** ................... category

**Aeby, Jacquelyn** ................ Regency
(a.k.a. Vanessa Gray)

**Aiken, Joan** .................... Regency/
(a.k.a. Joan Aiken Hodge)   romantic suspense

**Allister, Barbara** ................ category

**Allardyce, Paula** ................ Regency
(a.k.a. Ursula Torday)

**Alexander, Donna** ............... category
(a.k.a. Donna Vitek)

**Ames, Leslie** ..................... category
(a.k.a. Dan Ross, W. E. Daniel Ross,
Diana Randall, Marilyn Carter, Ann Gilmer,
Miriam Leslie, Ellen Randolph, Clarissa Ross,
Marilyn Ross, Jane Rossiter, Rose Williams)

**Anderson, Catherine** ....... Native American

**Anderson, Nina Romberg** ........ historical
(a.k.a. Jane Archer)

**Anderson, Roberta** .............. historical
(w/ Mary Kuczkir)
(a.k.a. Fern Michaels)

**Andrews, Felicia** ................ category
(a.k.a. Charles L. Grant)

**Andrews, Molly** ................. category
(a.k.a. Marti Jones, Martha J. Jones)

**Ansle, Dorothy Phoebe** ..... romantic suspense
(a.k.a Laura Conway)

**Anthony, Evelyn** .......... romantic suspense
(a.k.a. Evelyn Ward-Thomas)

**Archer, Jane** .................... historical
(a.k.a. Nina Romberg Anderson)

**Arthur, Lee** ......................category
(a.k.a. Lee and Arthur Browning)

**Astley, Juliet** .......historical/romantic suspense
(a.k.a. Norah Lufts, Peter Curtis)

| AUTHOR/pseudonyms | GENRE |
|---|---|

**Aston, Sharon** . . . . . . . . . . . . . . . . mainstream
(a.k.a. Helen Van Slyke)

**Auel, Jean** . . . . . . . . . . . . . . . . . . sci fi/fantasy

**August, Elizabeth** . . . . . . . . . . . . . . . . . category
(a.k.a. Betsy Page, Elizabeth Douglas,
Bettie Marie Wilhite)

**Austen, Jane** . . . . . . . . . . . . . . . . . . . . . . classic

**Avery, Anne** . . . . . . . . . . . . . . . . . . . . . category

**Backus, Carol Suzanne** . . . . . . . . . . . . historical
(a.k.a. Suzanne Barclay)

**Baier, Anna Lee** . . . . . . . . . . . . . . . . . category
(a.k.a. Ana Leigh)

**Baker, Madeline** . . . . . . . . . . . . . . . . time travel

**Bale, Karen A.** . . . . . . . . . . . . . . . . . . historical

**Balogh, Mary** . . . . . . . . . . . . . . . . . . . . regency

**Banks, Leanne** . . . . . . . . . . . . . . . . . . category

**Bannister, Patricia** . . . . . . . . . . . . . . . . regency
(a.k.a. Patricia Veryan)

**Barbieri, Elaine** . . . . . . . . . . . . . . . . . historical
(a.k.a. Elaine Rome)

**Barbour, Anne** . . . . . . . . . . . . . . . . . . category
(a.k.a. Barbara Yirka)

**Barclay, Suzanne** . . . . . . . . . . . . . . . . historical
(a.k.a. Carol Suzanne Backus)

**Barker, Megan** . . . . . . . . . . . . . . . . . . category
(a.k.a. Roger Longrigg)

**Barkin, Jill** . . . . . . . . . . . . . . . . contemporary
(a.k.a. Susan Johnson)

**Barnard, Judith** . . . . . . . . . . . . hist/mainstream
(w/ Michael Fain)
(a.k.a. Judith Michael)

**Barnett, Jill** . . . . . . . . . . . . . . . . . . . historical
(a.k.a. Jill Stadler)

**Barrie, Monica** . . . . . . . . . . . . . . . . . . category
(a.k.a. David Wind, Gena Dalton, Jenifer Dalton)

**Bartlett, Lynn** . . . . . . . . . . . . . . . . . . historical

**Barton, Beverly** . . . . . . . . . . . . . . . . . category
(a.k.a. Beverly Beaver)

**Baumgardner, Cathie Linz** . . . . . . . . . historical
(a.k.a. Cathie Linz)

**Beaver, Beverly** . . . . . . . . . . . . . . . . . category
(a.k.a. Beverly Barton)

**Beaumont, Nina** . . . . . . . . . . . . . . . . . category
(a.k.a. Nina Gettler)

| AUTHOR/pseudonyms | GENRE |
|---|---|

**Becnel, Rexanne** . . . . . . . . . . . . . . . . category
**Bell, Currer** . . . . . . . . . . . . . . . . . . . . . classic
   (a.k.a. Charlotte Brönte)
**Bell, Ellis** . . . . . . . . . . . . . . . . . . . . . . . classic
   (a.k.a. Emily Brönte)
**Bennett, Connie** . . . . . . . . . . . . . . . . . category
   (a.k.a. Constance Bennett)
**Bennett, Constance** . . . . . . . . . . . . . . category
   (a.k.a. Connie Bennett)
**Bennett, Emma** . . . . . . . . . . . . . . . . . category
   (a.k.a. Emma Merritt)
**Benson, Angela D.** . . . . . . . . . . . . . . . . category
**Benson, Margaret** . . . . . . . . . . . . . . . . category
   (a.k.a Maggie Shayne)
**Bentley, Jayne** . . . . . . . . . . . . . . . . . . category
   (a.k.a. Jayne Ann Krentz, Jayne Taylor,
   Amanda Glass, Jayne Castle,
   Amanda Quick, Stephanie James)
**Berland, Nancy** . . . . . . . . . . . . . . . . . . category
   (a.k.a. Nancy Landon)
**Beverley, Jo** . . . . . . . . . . . . . . . . . . . . . category
**Bicos, Olga** . . . . . . . . . . . . . . . . . . . . . category
   (a.k.a. Olga Gonzales-Bicos)
**Bieber, Janet** . . . . . . . . . . . . . . . . . . . category
(w/ Joyce Theis)
   (a.k.a. Janet Joyce)
**Biggs, Cheryl** . . . . . . . . . . . time travel/category
   (a.k.a. Cheryl Jac)
**Bittner, Roseanne** . . . . . . . . . . . . . . . . historical
**Blake, Jennifer** . . . . . . . . . . . . . . . . . . historical
   (a.k.a. Patricia Maxwell)
**Blake, Stephanie** . . . . . . . . . . . . . . . . category
   (a.k.a. Jack Pearl)
**Blanshard, Audrey** . . . . . . . . . . . . . . . . regency
**Blayne, Diana** . . . . . . . . . . . . . . . . . . . category
   (a.k.a. Diana Palmer, Kate Curry, Susan Kyle)
**Bonander, Jane** . . . . . . . . . . . . . . . . . . category
**Boswell, Barbra** . . . . . . . . . . . . . contemporary
   (a.k.a. Betsy Osborne)
**Bradshaw, Emily** . . . . . . . . . . . . . . . . . category
   (a.k.a. Emily Carmichael, Emily Kvokocz)
**Bradshaw, Valerie** . . . . . . . . . historical/category
   (a.k.a. Mary Linn Roby, Pamela D'Arcy, Georgina
   Grey, Pauline Pryor, Elisabeth Welles, Mary Wilson)

**Bramwell, L. E.** . . . . . . . . . . . . . contemporary
(a.k.a. Hope Goodwin, Linda Lee)

**Bremer, JoAnne** . . . . . . . . . . . . . . . . category
(w/ Carol I. Wagner)
(a.k.a. Joellyn Carroll)

**Brönte, Charlotte** . . . . . . . . . . . . . . . . classic
(a.k.a. Currer Bell)

**Brönte, Emily** . . . . . . . . . . . . . . . . . . . . classic
(a.k.a. Ellis Bell)

**Brönte, Louisa** . . . . . . . . . . . . . . . . . . . category
(a.k.a. Jane & Louise Roberts,
Janette Radcliffe, Rebecca Danton)

**Brookes, Beth** . . . . . . . . . . . . . . . . . . . category
(a.k.a. Lindsay McKenna, Eileen Nauman)

**Brooks, Janice Young** . . . . . . . . . . . . . category
(w/ Jean Brooks-Janowiak)
(a.k.a. Valerie Vayle)

**Brooks-Janowiak, Jean** . . . . . . . . . . . . category
(w/ Janice Young Brooks)
(a.k.a. Valerie Vayle)

**Broude, Craig Howard** . . . . . . . . . . . . category
(a.k.a. Lisa Lenore)

**Brouder, Greg** . . . . . . . . . . . . . . . . . . category
(w/ Diane Brouder)
(a.k.a. Lydia Gregory)

**Brouder, Diane** . . . . . . . . . . . . . . . . . . category
(w/ Greg Brouder)
(a.k.a. Lydia Gregory)

**Brown, Diana** . . . . . . . . . . . . . . . . . . . . regency

**Brown, Lisa G.** . . . . . . . . . . . . . . . . . . category
(a.k.a. Dana Warren Smith)

**Brown, Sandra** . . . . . . . . . . . mainstream/category
(a.k.a. Laura Jordan, Erin St. Clair, Rachel Ryan)

**Browning, Lee and Arthur** . . . . . . . . . . category
(a.k.a. Lee Arthur)

**Brownley, Margaret** . . . . . . . . . . . . . . category
(a.k.a. Megan Brownley, Kate Damon)

**Brownley, Megan** . . . . . . . . . . . . . . . . category
(a.k.a. Margaret Brownley, Kate Damon)

**Bucholtz, Eileen** . . . . . . . . . . . . . . . . . category
(a.k.a. Alyssa Howard, Alexis Hill Jordan,
Ruth Glick, Louise Titchenor)

COLLECTING ROMANCE NOVELS

| AUTHOR/pseudonyms | GENRE |

**Buckingham, Nancy** .............. category
(w/ John Sawyer)
(a.k.a. Nancy John)

**Buloch, Lynn** ................... category

**Bunkley, Anita Richmond** ......... category

**Burchell, Mary** .................. category
(a.k.a. Ida Cook)

**Burke, Cinnamon** ............... historical
(a.k.a. Phoebe Conn)

**Burke, Diana** .................... category
(a.k.a. Sue Burrell and Michaela Karni)

**Burrell, Sue** ..................... category
(w/ Michaela Karni)
(a.k.a. Diana Burke)

**Busbee, Shirlee** ................. historical

**Bush, Kim Ostrom** .............. category
(a.k.a. Kim Cates, Kimberly Cates)

**Butler, Gwendoline** ........ romantic suspense
(a.k.a. Jennie Melville)

**Butler, Rae** ..................... category
(a.k.a. Raymond Butler)

**Butler, Raymond** ................ category
(a.k.a. Rae Butler)

**Buxton, Anne** ........... romantic suspense
(a.k.a. Ann Maybury)

**Cajio, Linda** .................... category

**Caldwell, Anne** .................. category

**Caldwell, Pamela** ................ category

**Caldwell, Taylor** ................ historical
(a.k.a. Taylor Caldwell Prestie)

**Cameron, Charla** ................ category
(a.k.a. Gloria Dale Skinner)

**Cameron, Gay** .....................category

**Cameron, June** ................... category
(a.k.a. Sharon Ihle, Sharon MacIver)

**Cameron, Stella and Virginia Myers** . category
(a.k.a. Jane Worth Abbott)

**Camp, Candace** ................. historical
(a.k.a. Lisa Gregory, Kristin James)

**Campbell, Marilyn** ............... futuristic
(a.k.a. Marina Palmieri)

**Candlish, Jasmine** . . . . . . . . . . . . . . . . . category
(a.k.a. Jasmine Craig, Jasmine Cresswell)

**Cane, Nancy** . . . . . . . . . . . . . . . . . . futuristic
(a.k.a. Nancy Cohen)

**Canham, Marsha** . . . . . . . . . . . . . . . . . category

**Canon, Jack** . . . . . . . . . . . . . . . . . . . . .category
(w/ Mary Canon)
(a.k.a. Mary Canon)

**Canon, Mary** . . . . . . . . . . . . . . . . . . . . category
(a.k.a. Mary and Jack Canon)

**Cantrell, Raine** . . . . . . . . . . . . . . . . . historical
(a.k.a. Theresa Michaels, Theresa DiBenedetto)

**Carberry, Ann** . . . . . . . . . . . . . . . contemporary
(a.k.a. Maureen Child, Kathleen Kane)

**Carles, Riva** . . . . . . . . . . . . . . . . . . . . . category
(a.k.a. Irving Greenfield, Alicia Grace)

**Carlson, Janice** . . . . . . . . . . . . . . . . . . category
(a.k.a. Ashland Price)

**Carlyle, Tena** . . . . . . . . . . . . . . . . . . . category
(a.k.a. Ellen Lyle Taber and Carol Card Otten)

**Carmichael, Emily** . . . . . . . . . . . . . . . . category
(a.k.a. Emily Bradshaw, Emily Kvokocz)

**Carmichael, Jeanne** . . . . . . . . . . . . . . . regency
(a.k.a. Carol Michaels, Carol Quinto)

**Carr, Philippa** . . . . . . . . . . . romantic suspense/
(a.k.a. Victoria Holt,                 historical
Jean Plaidy, Eleanor Burford Hibbert)

**Carroll, Joellyn** . . . . . . . . . . . . . . . . . . category
(a.k.a. JoAnne Bremer and Carol I. Wagner)

**Carter, Marilyn** . . . . . . . . . . . . . . . . . . category
(a.k.a. Dan Ross, W. E. Daniel Ross, Leslie Ames,
Ann Gilmer, Miriam Leslie, Ellen Randolph,
Clarissa Ross, Marilyn Ross, Jane Rossiter,
Rose Williams)

**Cartland, Barbara** . . . . . . . . . . . . . . . . regency

**Castle, Jayne** . . . . . . . . . . . . . . . . . . . . category
(a.k.a. Jayne Ann Krentz, Jayne Bentley,
Jayne Taylor, Amanda Glass,
Amanda Quick, Stephanie James)

**Castle, Linda** . . . . . . . . . . . . . . . . . . . category

**Castle, Philippa** . . . . . . . . . . . . . . . . . regency
(a.k.a. Marilyn M. Lowery)

**Cates, Kim** . . . . . . . . . . . . . . . . . . . . . category
(a.k.a. Kimberly Cates, Kim Ostrom Bush)

**Cates, Kimberly** . . . . . . . . . . . . . . . category
(a.k.a. Kim Cates, Kim Ostrom Bush)

**Catlin, Barbara** . . . . . . . . . . . . . . . . . category
(a.k.a. Barbara Catlin Craven)

**Caulder, Inglath** . . . . . . . . . . . . . . . category
(a.k.a. Inglath Cooper)

**Cavanaugh, Helen** . . . . . . . . . . . . . . category

**Chase, Elaine Raco** . . . . . . . . . . . . . . category

**Chastain, Sandra** . . . . . . . . . category/historical
(a.k.a. Jenna Darcy, Allie Jordan)

**Chesney, Marion** . . . . . . . . . . . category/regency
(a.k.a. Jennie Tremaine, Ann Fairfax,
Helen Crampton, Marion Chesney Gibbons)

**Child, Maureen** . . . . . . . . . . . . . . contemporary
(a.k.a. Ann Carberry, Kathleen Kane)

**Childress, Susan** . . . . . . . . . . . . . . . historical
(a.k.a. Susan Wiggs)

**Christopher, Paula** . . . . . . . . . . . . . . category
(a.k.a. Lynn Michaels, Lynn A. Smith)

**Cichanth, Elaine** . . . . . . . . . . . . . . . . category
(w/ Elizabeth Schaal, Elizabeth Shelley)

**Civil, Susan** . . . . . . . . . . . . . . . . . . . category
(a.k.a. Rachel Lee)

**Clare, Cathleen** . . . . . . . . . . . . . . . . category
(a.k.a. Catherine Ann Toothman)

**Clark, Christie** . . . . . . . . . . . . . . . . . category
(a.k.a. Christie Craig)

**Clark, Gail** . . . . . . . . . . . . . . . . . . . regency
(a.k.a. Maggie MacKeever)

**Claybourne, Casey** . . . . . . . . . . . . . . category
(a.k.a. Casey Mickle)

**Clayton, Donna** . . . . . . . . . . . . . . . . category
(a.k.a. Donna Fasano)

**Cleaves, Margaret Major** . . . . . . . . . . .category
(a.k.a. Ann Major)

**Coffman, Elaine** . . . . . . . . . . . . . . contemporary

**Coffman, Virginia Edith** . . . . . . . . . . . . gothic
(a.k.a. Victor Cross, Virginia Deuvaul,
Jeanne Duval, Diana Saunders, Ann Stanfield)

**Cohen, Nancy** . . . . . . . . . . . . . . . . . futuristic
(a.k.a. Nancy Cane)

**Cole, Justine** . . . . . . . . . . . . . . . . . . category
(a.k.a. Claire Kiehl and Susan Phillips)

**Collins, Susanna** . . . . . . . . . . . . . . . . . category
  (a.k.a. Sue Ellen Gross)
**Comstock, Mary Chase** . . . . . . . . . . . category
**Conaway, James** . . . . . . . . . . . . . . . . . category
  (a.k.a. Debrah Lewis, Leila Lyons)
**Conlee, Jaelyn** . . . . . . . . . . . . . . . . . category
  (a.k.a. Fayrene Preston)
**Conn, Phoebe** . . . . . . . . . . . . . . . . . . category
  (a.k.a. Cinnamon Burke)
**Conway, Laura** . . . . . . . . . . . romantic suspense
  (a.k.a. Dorothy Phoebe Ansle)
**Cook, Ida** . . . . . . . . . . . . . . . . . . . . . category
  (a.k.a. Mary Burchell)
**Cook, S. A.** . . . . . . . . . . . . . . . . contemporary
  (a.k.a. Lacy Dancer)
**Cooke, Deborah A. Kennedy** . . . . . . . . historical
  (a.k.a. Claire Delacroix)
**Coombs, Ann** . . . . . . . . . . . . . . . . category/
  (a.k.a. Nina Pykare,                     contemporary
  Nina Coombs, Nan Pemberton,
  Nina Porter, Nora Powers, Regina Towers)
**Coombs, Nina** . . . . . . . . . . . . . . . . category/
  (a.k.a. Ann Coombs,                      contemporary
  Nina Pykare, Nan Pemberton,
  Nina Porter, Nora Powers, Regina Towers)
**Cooper, Inglath** . . . . . . . . . . . . . . . . category
  (a.k.a. Inglath Caulder)
**Cookson, Catherine** . . . . . category/mainstream
  (a.k.a. Catherine Marchant, Katie McMullen)
**Copeland, Lori** . . . . . . . . . . . . . . . . . category
**Corcoran, Dotty** . . . . . . . . . . . . . . . . category
  (w/ Mary Ann Slojkowski) (a.k.a. DeAnn Patrick)
**Cothran, Betty** . . . . . . . . . . . . . . . . . category
**Coulter, Catherine** . . . . . . . . . category/regency
**Cowan, Debra S.** . . . . . . . . . . . . . . . . category
**Coy, Stanlee** . . . . . . . . . . . . . . . . . . category
  (a.k.a. Cissie Miller)
**Craig, Christie** . . . . . . . . . . . . . . . . . category
  (a.k.a. Christie Clark)
**Craig, Jasmine** . . . . . . . . . . . . . . . . . category
  (a.k.a. Jasmine Cresswell, Jasmine Candlish)
**Crampton, Helen** . . . . . . . . . . category/regency
  (a.k.a. Marion Chesney, Jennie Tremain,
  Ann Fairfax, Marion Chesney Gibbons)

**Crane, Leah** . . . . . . . . . . . . . . . . . . . category/
  (a.k.a. Jean Hager,          Native American
  Marlaine Kyle, Jeanne Stephens)

**Craven, Barbara Catlin** . . . . . . . . . . . category
  (a.k.a. Barbara Catlin)

**Crawford, Diane** . . . . . . . . . . . . . contemporary
  (a.k.a. Georgette Livingston, Camille Crawford)

**Cresswell, Jasmine** . . . . . . . . . . . . . . . category
  (a.k.a. Jasmine Craig, Jasmine Candlish)

**Cristy, Ann** . . . . . . . . . . . . . . . . . . . category
  (a.k.a. Hayton Monteith, Helen Mittermeyer)

**Criswell, Millie** . . . . . . . . . . . . . . . . historical

**Croissant, Kay** . . . . . . . . . . . . . . . . . category
(w/ Catherine Dee)
  (a.k.a. Catherine Kay)

**Crosby, Tanya Anne** . . . . . . . . . . . . . . category

**Cross, Charlene** . . . . . . . . . . . . . . . . category

**Cross, Victor** . . . . . . . . . . . . . . category/gothic
  (a.k.a. Virginia Edith Coffman, Virginia Deuval,
  Jeanne Duval, Diana Saunders, Ann Stanfield)

**Crowleigh, Ann** . . . . . . . . . mainstream/category
  (a.k.a. Barbara Cummings and JoAnn Power)

**Cummings, Barbara** . . . . . mainstream/category
(w/ JoAnn Power)
  (a.k.a. Ann Crowleigh)

**Curry, Kate** . . . . . . . . . . . . . . . . . inspirational
  (a.k.a. Diana Palmer, Diana Blayne, Susan Kyle)

**Curtis, Peter** . . . . . . .historical/romantic suspense
              (a.k.a. Norah Lufts, Julie Astley)

**Curtis, Sharon/Tom** . . . . . . . . . . . . . . category
  (a.k.a. Robin James, Laura London)

**Dailey, Janet** . . . . . . . . . . category/mainstream/
                 historical/contemporary

**Dalton, Gena** . . . . . . . . . . . . . . . . . . category
  (a.k.a. David Wind, Monica Barrie, Jenifer Dalton)

**Dalton, Jenifer** . . . . . . . . . . . . . . . . . category
  (a.k.a. Gena Dalton, David Wind, Monica Barrie)

**Damon, Kate** . . . . . . . . . . . . . . . . . . category
  (a.k.a. Margaret Brownley, Megan Brownley)

**Dancer, Lacy** . . . . . . . . . . . . . . . . . . category
  (a.k.a. S. A. Cook)

**Daniel, Megan** . . . . . . . . . . . . . . . . . regency

**Daniels, Joleen** . . . . . . . . . . . . . . contemporary
  (a.k.a. Gayle Malone Schimek)

**Daniels, Maggie** . . . . . . . . . . . . . . . . historical
(a.k.a. Maggie Davis, Katherine Deauxville)

**Danton, Rebecca** . . . . . . . . . . category/regency
(a.k.a. Janet Louise Roberts,
Janette Radcliffe, Louisa Brönte)

**Daoust, Pamela** . . . . . . . . . . . . . . . . category
(a.k.a. Katharine Kincaid)

**D'Arcy, Pamela** . . . . . . . . . . . . . . . . . category
(a.k.a. Georgia Grey, Pauline Pryor,
Elisabeth Welles, Mary Wilson,
Valerie Bradshaw, Mary Linn Roby)

**Darcy, Clare** . . . . . . . . . . . . . . . . . . . . regency

**Darcy, Jenna** . . . . . . . . . . . . . category/historical
(a.k.a. Sandra Chastain, Allie Jordan)

**Davenport, Kathryn** . . . . . . . . . . . . . . category
(a.k.a. Keller Graves, Evelyn Rogers)

**Davidson, Sandra** . . . . . . . historical/time travel

**Davis, Justine** . . . . . . . . . . . . . . . . . . category

**Davis, Maggie** . . . . . . . . . . . . category/historical
(a.k.a. Katherine Deauxville, Maggie Daniels)

**Deauxville, Katherine** . . . . . . . . . . . . . historical
(a.k.a. Maggie Daniels, Maggie Davis)

**de Covarrubias, Barbara Faith** . . . . . . . . category
(a.k.a. Barbara Faith)

**Dees, Catherine** . . . . . . . . . . . . . . . . . category
(w/ Kay Croissant)
(a.k.a. Catherine Kay)

**Delacroix, Claire** . . . . . . . . . . . . . . . . historical
(a.k.a. Deborah A. Kennedy Cooke)

**de la Fuente, Patricia** . . . . . . . . . . . . . category
(a.k.a. Patricia Oliver, Olivia Fontayne)

**DeLezzari, JoAnn** . . . . . . . . . . . . . . . .category

**Delinsky, Barbara** . . . . . . category/mainstream
(a.k.a. Bonnie Drake, Billie Douglass)

**DeSha, Sandra Donovan** . . . . . . . . . . category
(a.k.a. Sandra Donovan)

**Deuvaul, Virginia** . . . . . . . . . . category/gothic
(a.k.a. Virginia Edith Coffman, Victor Cross,
Jeanne Duval, Diana Saunders, Ann Standfield)

**Devereaux, Jude** . . . . . . . . . . . . . . . . historical

**Devine, Thea** . . . . . . . . . . . . . . . . . . . category

**Diamond, Graham** . . . . . . . . . . . . . . . category
(a.k.a. Rochelle Leslie)

**Duval, Jeanne** . . . . . . . . . . . . . . category/gothic
(a.k.a. Virginia Edith Coffman, Victor Cross,
Virginia Deuval, Diana Saunders, Ann Stanfield)

**Eagle, Kathleen** . . . . . . . . . . . . . . . . . historical

**Eberhart, Mignon** . . . . . . . . romantic suspense

**Eden, Dorothy** . . . . . . . . . romantic suspense
(a.k.a. Mary Paradise)

**Edwards, Cassie** . . . . . . . . . . . . . . historical

**Elliott, Anne** . . . . . . . . . . . . . . . . . . . . category
(w/ Christina Dorsey)
(a.k.a. Christina Elliott)

**Elliott, Christina** . . . . . . . . . . . . . . . . category
(a.k.a. Anne Elliott and Christina Dorsey)

**Elliott, Robin** . . . . . . . . . . . . . . . . . . category
(a.k.a. Joan Elliott Pickart)

**Ellis, Lyn** . . . . . . . . . . . . . . . . . . . . . . category

**Elward, James** . . . . . . . . . . . . . . . . . . category
(a.k.a. Rebecca James)

**Emerson, Kathy Lynn** . . . . . . . . . . . category
(a.k.a. Kaitlyn Gordon)

**Erickson, Lynn** . . . . . . . . . . . . . . . . . category
(a.k.a. Carla Peltonen and Molly Swanson)

**Erskine, Helen** . . . . . young adult/contemporary
(a.k.a. Helen Santori)

**Estrada, Rita Clay** . . . . . . . . . . . . . . category
(a.k.a. Linda King Ladd)

**Evanovich, Janet** . . . . . . . . . . . . . . . . category
(a.k.a. Steffie Hall)

**Fairfax, Ann** . . . . . . . . . . . . . . regency/category
(a.k.a. Marion Chesney, Helen Crampton,
Marion Chesney Gibbons, Jennie Tremaine)

**Faith, Barbara** . . . . . . . . . . . . . . . . . . category
(a.k.a. Barbara Faith deCovarrubias)

**Fasana, Donna** . . . . . . . . . . . . . . . . . category
(a.k.a. Donna Clayton)

**Feather, Jane** . . . . . . . . . . . . . . . . . historical
(a.k.a. Claudia Bishop)

**Fedderson, Connie** . . . . . . . . . . . . . . category
(a.k.a. Carol Finch, Connie Drake, Gina Robins)

**Field, Sandra** . . . . . . . . . . . . . . . . . . category
(w/ Anne MacLean)
(a.k.a. Jan MacLean, Jocelyn Haley)

**Finch, Carol** . . . . . . . . . . . . . . . . . . category
(a.k.a. Connie Fedderson,
Connie Drake, Gina Robins)

**Fireside, Carolyn** . . . . . . . . . . . . contemporary
(a.k.a. Joanne Burgess)

**Fitzgerald, Julia** . . . . . . . . . . . . . . . . historical
(a.k.a. Julia Watson)

**Fontayne, Olivia** . . . . . . . . . . . . . . . . . category
(a.k.a. Patricia Oliver, Patricia de la Fuente)

**Forster, Suzanne** . . . . . . . . . . . . . . . category

**Foxx, Rosalind** . . . . . . . . . . . . . . . . . . category
(a.k.a. June Hayden and Judith Simpson, Sara Logan)

**Gabaldon, Diana** . . . . . . . . . . . . . . . . category

**Gaffney, Patricia** . . . . . . . . . . . . . . . . category

**Gallagher, Patricia** . . . . . . . . . . . . . historical

**Gallant, Jennie** . . . . . . . . . . . . . . . . . . regency
(a.k.a. Joan Smith)

**Garcia, Marietta Kay** . . . . . . . . . . . historical
(a.k.a. Elizabeth Mayne)

**Gardner, Kit** . . . . . . . . . . . . . . . . . . . . category
(a.k.a. Katherine Manning Garland)

**Garland, Katherine Manning** . . . . . . . category
(a.k.a. Kit Gardner)

**Garlock, Dorothy** . . . . . . . . . . . . . . . . category
(a.k.a. Dorothy Glenn,
Dorothy Phillips, Joanna Phillips)

**Garrett, Wendy** . . . . . . . . . . . . . . . . . category
(a.k.a. Wendy Haley)

**Garwood, Julie** . . . . . . . . . . . . . . contemporary

**Gaskin, Catherine** . . . . . . . . . romantic suspense

**Gellis, Roberta** . . . . . . . . . . . . . . . . . historical
(a.k.a. Priscilla Hamilton)

**Gentry, Georgina** . . . . . . . . . Native American
(a.k.a. Lynne Murphy)

**George, Teresa** . . . . . . . . . . . . . . . . . . category
(a.k.a. Teresa Howard)

**Gettler, Nina** . . . . . . . . . . . . . . . . . . . category
(a.k.a. Nina Beaumont)

**Gibbons, Marion Chesney** . . . category/regency
(a.k.a. Marion Chesney, Ann Fairfax,
Helen Crampton, Jennie Tremaine)

**Giddings, Lauren** . . . . . . . . . . . . contemporary
(a.k.a. Nancy Gideon, Dana Ransom)

**Gideon, Nancy** . . . . . . . . . . . . . . contemporary
(a.k.a. Lauren Giddings, Dana Ransom)

**Gilbert, Laurie** . . . . . . . . . . . . . . . . . . category
(a.k.a. Laurie Walker)

**Gillis, Jackie** . . . . . . . . . . . . regency/historical

**Gilmer, Ann** . . . . . . . . . . . . . . . . . . . . . category
(a.k.a. Dan Ross, Marilyn Carter,
W. E. Daniel Ross, Leslie Ames,
Miriam Leslie, Ellen Randolph, Clarissa Ross,
Marilyn Ross, Jane Rossiter, Rose Williams)

**Gladden, Theresa** . . . . . . . . . . . . . . . . category

**Gladstone, Arthur** . . . . . . . . . . . . . . . category
(a.k.a. Maggie Gladstone, Elisabet Norcross,
Margaret Sebastian)

**Gladstone, Maggie** . . . . . . . . . . . . . . . category
(a.k.a. Arthur Gladstone, Elisabet Norcross,
Margaret Sebastian)

**Glass, Amanda** . . . . . . . . . . . . . category/fantasy
(a.k.a. Jayne Anne Krentz, Jayne Bentley, Jayne Castle,
Amanda Quick, Jayne Taylor, Stephanie James)

**Glenn, Dorothy** . . . . . . . . . . . . . . . . . category
(a.k.a. Dorothy Garlock,
Dorothy Phillips, Joanna Phillips)

**Glick, Ruth** . . . . . . . . . . . . . . . . . . . . . category
(a.k.a. Alyssa Howard, Louise Titchenor,
Alexis Hill Jordan, Eileen Bucholtz)

**Goldacker, Debra Dier** . . . . . . . . . . . category
(a.k.a. Debra Dier)

**Golon, Sergeanne** . . . . . . . . . . . . . . . historical

**Gonzales-Bicos, Olga** . . . . . . . . . . . . category
(a.k.a. Olga Bicos)

**Goodman, Irene** . . . . . . . . . . . . . . . . . category
(w/ Alex Kamaroff)
(a.k.a. Diane Morgan)

**Goodwin, Hope** . . . . . . . . . . . . . .contemporary
(a.k.a. Linda Lee, L. E. Bramwell)

**Gordon, Debbie Brooke** . . . . . . .contemporary
(a.k.a. Brooke Hastings)

**Gordon, Kaitlyn** . . . . . . . . . . . . . . . . . category
(a.k.a. Kathy Lynn Emerson)

**Gottlieg, Irene Hannon** . . . . . . . . . . . category
(a.k.a. Irene Hannon)

**Goulart, Ron** . . . . . . . . . . . . . . . . . . . . category
(a.k.a. Jill Kearny)

**Grace, Alicia** . . . . . . . . . . . . . . . . . . . . category
(a.k.a. Riva Carles, Irving Greenfield)

**Graham, Heather** . . . . . . . . . category/historical
(a.k.a. Heather Graham Pozzessere, Shannon Drake)

| AUTHOR/*pseudonyms* | GENRE |
|---|---|

**Grant, Anna** . . . . . . . . . . . . . . . . . . . . category
  (a.k.a. Tracy Grant and Joan Grant,
  Anthea Malcolm)

**Grant, Charles L.** . . . . . . . . . . . . . . . . category
  (a.k.a. Felicia Andrews)

**Grant, Joan** . . . . . . . . . . . . . . . . . . . . . category
(w/ Tracy Grant)
  (a.k.a. Anna Grant, Anthea Malcolm)

**Grant, Tracy** . . . . . . . . . . . . . . . . . . . . category
(w/ Joan Grant)
  (a.k.a. Anna Grant, Anthea Malcolm)

**Granville, Louise** . . . . . . . . . . . . . . . . category
  (a.k.a. Anne Griffin, Arthur Griffin)

**Graves, Keller** . . . . . . . . . . . . . . . . . . category
  (a.k.a. Evelyn Rogers, Kathryn Davenport)

**Gray, Ginna** . . . . . . . . . . . . . . . . . . . . . category

**Gray, Vanessa** . . . . . . . . . . . . . . . . . . . regency
  (a.k.a. Jacquelyn Aeby)

**Grayson, Elizabeth** . . . . . . . . . . . . . . . category
  (a.k.a. Elizabeth Kary)

**Grayson, Leanne** . . . . . . . . . . . . . . . . category
  (a.k.a. Robin Lee Wiete)

**Greenberg, Jan** . . . . . . . . . . . . . . . . . . category
  (a.k.a. Jill Gregory)

**Greenfield, Irving** . . . . . . . . . . . . . . . . category
  (a.k.a. Riva Carles, Alicia Grace)

**Greenwood, Leigh** . . . . . . . . . . . . . . . category
  (a.k.a. Harold Lowry)

**Gregory, Jill** . . . . . . . . . . . . . . . . . . . . category
  (a.k.a. Jan Greenberg)

**Gregory, Lisa** . . . . . . . . . . . . . . . . . . . historical
  (a.k.a. Candace Camp)

**Gregory, Lydia** . . . . . . . . . . . . . . . . . . category
  (a.k.a. Diane and Greg Brouder)

**Grey, Georgina** . . . . . . . . . . . . . . . . . category/
  (a.k.a. Pauline Pryor, Elisabeth Welles,    historical
  Mary Wilson, Pamela D'Arcy, Mary Linn Roby,
  Valerie Bradshaw)

**Grieveson, Mildred** . . . . . . . . . . . . . . category
  (a.k.a. Anne Mather)

**Griffin, Anne** . . . . . . . . . . . . . . . . . . . category
  (a.k.a. Louise Granville, Arthur Griffin)

**Gross, Sue Ellen** . . . . . . . . . . . . . . . . .category
  (a.k.a. Susanna Collins)

**AUTHOR/pseudonyms**                                          GENRE

**Guntrum, Suzanne Simmons** . . . . . . . . . category
(a.k.a. Suzanne Simms)

**Haddad, Sandi** . . . . . . . . . . . . . . contemporary

**Haeger, Diane** . . . . . . . . . . . . . . . . . category

**Hager, Jean** . . . . . . . . . . . . . . Native American
(a.k.a. Leah Crane, Marlaine Kyle, Jeanne Stephens)

**Haley, Wendy** . . . . . . . . . . . . . . . . . . . . category
(a.k.a. Wendy Garrett)

**Hall, Libby** . . . . . . . . . . . . . . . . . . . . . . category
(a.k.a. Laurie Paige, Olivia M. Hall)

**Hall, Olivia M.** . . . . . . . . . . . . . . . . . . category
(a.k.a. Libby Hall, Laurie Paige)

**Hall, Steffie** . . . . . . . . . . . . . . . . . . . . category
(a.k.a. Janet Evanovich)

**Halliday, Sylvia** . . . . . . . . . . . . . . . . . . category
(a.k.a. Louisa Rawlings, Sylvia Baumgarten)

**Hallin, Emily** . . . . . . . . . . . . . . . . . young adult
(a.k.a. Elaine Harper)

**Halsall, Penny** . . . . . . . . . . . . . . . . . . . category
(a.k.a. Penny Jordan)

**Hampson, Anne** . . . . . . . . . . . . . . . . . category

**Hannon, Irene** . . . . . . . . . . . . . . . . . . category
(a.k.a. Irene Hannon Gottlieg)

**Harding-Pollero, Rhonda** . . . . . . . . . . category
(a.k.a. Kelsey Roberts)

**Hardy, Laura** . . . . . . . . . . . . category/historical
(a.k.a. Charlotte Lamb, Sheila Holland)

**Harper, Elaine** . . . . . . . . . . . . . . . . young adult
(a.k.a. Emily Hallin)

**Harper, Madeline** . . . . . . . . . category/historical
(a.k.a. Madeline Porter and Shannon Harper)

**Harper, Shannon** . . . . . . . . . category/historical
(w/ Madeline Porter)
    (a.k.a. Madeline Harper,
    Elizabeth Habersham, Anne James)

**Harrell, Anne** . . . . . . . . . . . category/mainstream/
(a.k.a. Carla/           romantic suspense
Carla A. Neggers, Amalia James)

**Harrington, Kathleen** . . . . . . . . . . . . . category

**Hart, Catherine** . . . . . . . . . . . . . . . . . category

**Hastings, Brooke** . . . . . . . . . . . . . contemporary
(a.k.a. Debbie Brooke Gordon)

| AUTHOR/pseudonyms | GENRE |
|---|---|

**Hatcher, Robin Lee** . . . . . . . . . . . . . historical
  (a.k.a. Robin Leigh)

**Hayden, June** . . . . . . . . . . . . . . . . . . category
(w/ Judith Simpson)  (a.k.a. Rosalind Foxx)

**Healy, Christine** . . . . . . . . . . . . . . . . . category
(w/ Susan Yansick)  (a.k.a. Erin York)

**Heath, Lorraine** . . . . . . . . . . . . . . . historical
  (a.k.a. Jan Nowasky)

**Heck, Boni** . . . . . . . . . . . . . . . . . . . . category

**Heggan, Christiane** . . . . . . . . . . . . mainstream

**Helmer, Roberta** . . . . . . . . . . . . . . . . category
  (a.k.a. Christina Skye)

**Hendrickson, Dee** . . . . . . . . . . . . . . category
  (a.k.a. Emily Hendrickson)

**Hendrickson, Emily** . . . . . . . . . . . . . . category
  (a.k.a. Dee Hendrickson)

**Henke, Shirl** . . . . . . . . . . . . . . . . . . . category
  (a.k.a. Caroly Reynard)

**Henley, Virginia** . . . . . . . . . . . . . . . . historical

**Herrmann, Nira** . . . . . . . . . . . . . . . . category
(w/ Phyllis DiFrancesco)
  (a.k.a. Phyllis Herrmann)

**Herrmann, Phyllis** . . . . . . . . . . . . . . category
  (a.k.a. Nira Herrmann and Phyllis DiFrancesco)

**Heyer, Georgette** . . . . . . . . . . . . . . . . regency

**Hiatt, Brenda** . . . . . . . . . . . . . . . . . . category

**Hibbert, Eleanor Burford** . . . . . . . . romantic/
  (a.k.a. Jean Plaidy,          suspense/historical
  Philippa Carr, Victoria Holt)

**Hill, Fiona** . . . . . . . . . . . . . . . . . . . . . regency
  (a.k.a. Ellen Jane Pall)

**Hines, Jeanne** . . . . . . . . . . . . . . . . . historical
  (a.k.a. Valerie Sherwood)

**Hinkemeyer, Mike** . . . . . . . . . . . . . historical
  (a.k.a. Vanessa Royall)

**Hoag, Tami** . . . . . . . . . . . . . . . . . . . historical

**Hodge, Jane Aiken** . . . . . . . . . . . . . .regency/
  (a.k.a. Joan Aiken)          romantic suspense

**Hoffman, Kate** . . . . . . . . . . . . . . . . . category
  (a.k.a. Peggy Hoffmann)

**Hoffman, Peggy** . . . . . . . . . . . . . . . . category
  (a.k.a. Kate Hoffmann)

| AUTHOR/pseudonyms | GENRE |
|---|---|

**Hohl, Joan** . . . . . . . . . . . . . . . . . . . . . category
(a.k.a. Amii Lorin, Paula Roberts)

**Holland, Isabelle** . . . . . . . . . romantic suspense

**Holland, Sheila** . . . . . . . . . . category/historical
(a.k.a. Charlotte Lamb, Laura Hardy)

**Holt, Victoria** . . . . . . . . . . . . . . . . . . historical
(a.k.a. Philippa Carr,
Eleanor Burford Hibbert, Jean Plaidy)

**Hooper, Kay** . . . . . . . . . . . . . category/futuristic
(a.k.a. Kay Robbins)

**Hoos, Suzanne** . . . . . . . . . . . . . . . . . . category
(a.k.a. Antoinette Stockenberg)

**Howard, Alyssa** . . . . . . . . . . . . . . . . . . category
(a.k.a. Ruth Glick,
Louise Titchenor, Eileen Bucholtz)

**Howard, Jessica** . . . . . . . . . . . . . . . . . category
(a.k.a. Monroe and Jean Schere)

**Howard, Linda** . . . . . . . . . . . . . . . . . . category
(a.k.a. Linda Howlington)

**Howard, Teresa** . . . . . . . . . . . . . . . . . category
(a.k.a. Teresa George)

**Howatch, Susan** . . . . . . . . . . . . . . . mainstream

**Howell, Hannah** . . . . . . . . . . . . . . . . historical
(a.k.a. Anna Jennet, Sarah Dustin)

**Howlington, Linda** . . . . . . . . . . . . . . . category
(a.k.a. Linda Howard)

**Hrimak, Denise** . . . . . . . . . . . . . . . . . category
(w/ Pat Mathews)
(a.k.a. Denis Mathews)

**Hubbard, Charlotte** . . . . . . . . . . . . . . category

**Hudson, Jan** . . . . . . . . . . . . . . . . . . . . category
(a.k.a. Ellen Kelly)

**Hudson, Janece Oliver** . . . . . . . . . . . . category
(a.k.a. Jan Oliver)

**Hudson, Janis Reams** . . . . . . . . . . . . historical

**Huff, Tom E.** . . . . . . . . . . . . . . . . . . historical
(a.k.a. Jennifer Wilde)

**Ihle, Sharon** . . . . . . . . . . . . . . . . . . . category
(a.k.a. Sharon MacIver, June Cameron)

**Jac, Cheryl** . . . . . . . . . . . . . . . . . . . time travel
(a.k.a. Cheryl Biggs)

**Jackson, Angela and Sandra** . . . . category/ethnic
(a.k.a. Lisa Saunders)

| AUTHOR/pseudonyms | GENRE |
|---|---|

**James, Anna** . . . . . . . . . . . . . . . . . . . . category
(a.k.a. Madeline Porter and Shannon Harper)

**James, Amalia** . . . . . . . . . . . . . . . . . . category
(a.k.a. Carla Neggers, Anne Harrell)

**James, Deana** . . . . . . . . . . . . . . . . . . category
(a.k.a. Mona Sizer)

**James, Kristin** . . . . . . . . . . . . . . . . . . category
(a.k.a. Candace Camp, Lisa Gregory)

**James, Rebecca** . . . . . . . . . . . . . . . . . category
(a.k.a. James Elward)

**James, Robin** . . . . . . . . . . . . . . . . . . . category
(a.k.a. Laura London, Tom and Sharon Curtis)

**James, Stephanie** . . . . . . . . . . . . . . . . . fantasy/
(a.k.a. Jayne Castle, Jayne    category/historical
Ann Krentz, Amanda Glass,
Jayne Taylor, Amanda Quick, Jayne Bentley)

**Janssen, Krista** . . . . . . . . . . . . . . . . . category
(a.k.a. Rhoda Janssen Poole)

**Jarrett, Miranda** . . . . . . . . . . . . . . . . . historical
(a.k.a. Susan Holloway Scott)

**Jason, Veronica** . . . . . . . . . . . romantic suspense
(a.k.a. Velda Johnston)

**Jeffries, Julia** . . . . . . . . . Regency/contemporary
(a.k.a. Lynda Ward)

**Jennet, Anna** . . . . . . . . . . . . . . . . . . . historical
(a.k.a. Hannah Howell, Sarah Dustin)

**Johanson, Iris** . .category/historical/contemporary

**John, Nancy** . . . . . . . . . . . . . . . . . . . . category
(a.k.a. Nancy Buckingham and John Sawyer)

**Johnson, Susan** . . . . . . . . . . . . . . . contemporary
(a.k.a. Jill Barkin)

**Johnston, Joan** . . . . . . . . . . . . . . . . . . historical

**Johnston, Velda** . . . . . . . . . . romantic suspense
(a.k.a. Veronica Jason)

**Jones, Martha J.** . . . . . . . . . . . . . . . . . category
(a.k.a. Marti Jones, Molly Andrews)

**Jones, Marti** . . . . . . . . . . . . . . . . . . . . category
(a.k.a. Martha J. Jones, Molly Andrews)

**Jordan, Allie** . . . . . . . . . . . . category/historical
(a.k.a. Sandra Chastain, Jenny Darcy)

**Jordan, Alexis Hill** . . . . . . . . . . . . . . . category
(a.k.a. Ruth Glick and Louise Titchenor)

**Jordan, Laura** . . . . . . . . . . . . . . . . . . category
(a.k.a. Sandra Brown, Erin St. Clair, Rachel Ryan)

**Jordan, Penny** . . . . . . . . . . . . . . . . . . . category
(a.k.a. Penny Halsall)

**Joseph, Robert** . . . . . . . . . . . . . . . . . . category
(a.k.a. Robin Joseph)

**Joseph, Robin** . . . . . . . . . . . . . . . . . . . category
(a.k.a. Robert Joseph)

**Joyce, Brenda** . . . . . . . . historical/contemporary

**Joyce, Janet** . . . . . . . . . . . . . . . . . . . . . category
(a.k.a. Janet Bieber and Joyce Theis)

**Kachelmeier, Glenda** . . . . . . category/historical
(a.k.a. Glenda Sanders, Glenda Sands)

**Kamaroff, Alex and Goodman, Irene** . . category
(a.k.a. Diana Morgan)

**Kane, Andrea** . . . . . . . . . . . . . . . . . . . category

**Kane, Kathleen** . . . . . . . . . . . . . contemporary
(a.k.a. Maureen Child, Ann Carberry)

**Kapala, Robin** . . . . . . . . . . . . . . . . . . . category
(a.k.a. Robin Nicholas)

**Karni, Michaela** (w/ Sue Burrell) . . . . . category
(a.k.a. Diana Burke)

**Karr, Jillian** . . . . . . . . . . . . . . . . . . . . category

**Kary, Elizabeth** . . . . . . . . . . . . . . . . . category
(a.k.a. Karyn Whitmer-Gow)

**Kasey, Michelle** . . . . . . . . . . . . . . . . . category
(a.k.a. Kasey Michaels, Kathryn Seidick)

**Kauffman, Donna** . . . . . . . . . . . . . . . . category

**Kay, Catherine** . . . . . . . . . . . . . . . . . . category
(a.k.a. Catherine Dees and Kay Croissant)

**Kearny, Jill** . . . . . . . . . . . . . . . . . . . . . category
(a.k.a. Ron Goulart)

**Keelyn, Patricia** . . . . . . . . . . . . . . . . . category
(a.k.a. Pat Van Wie)

**Kelley, Dorsey** . . . . . . . . . . . . . . . . . category
(a.k.a. Dorsey Adams)

**Kelly, Ellen** . . . . . . . . . . . . . . . . . . . . category
(a.k.a. Jan Hudson)

**Kendall, Julia Jay** . . . . . . . . . . . . . . . category
(a.k.a. Katherine Kingsley)

**Kent, Fortune** . . . . . . . . . . . . . . . . . . category
(a.k.a. John Toombs, Jocelyn Wilde)

**Kerstan, Lynn** . . . . . . . . . . . . . . . . . . category

**Kidd, Flora** . . . . . . . . . . . . . . . . . . . . . category

**Kidder, Jane** (w/ Charla Chin)          category
(a.k.a. Charlotte Simms, Charlotte McPherren)

| AUTHOR/pseudonyms | GENRE |
|---|---|

**Kiehl, Claire** (w/ Susan Phillips)    category
(a.k.a. Justine Cane)

**Kimbro, John M.** . . . . . . . . . . . . . . . . .gothic
(a.k.a. Kathryn Kimbrough)

**Kimbrough, Kathryn** . . . . . . . . . . . . . . . gothic
(a.k.a. John M. Kimbro)

**Kincaid, Katherine** . . . . . . . . . . . . . . category
(a.k.a. Pamela Daoust)

**King, Susan** . . . . . . . . . . . . . . . . . . . . category

**Kingsley, Katherine** . . . . . . . . . . . . . . category
(a.k.a. Julia Jay Kendall)

**Kirk, Alexandra** . . . . . . . . . . . .suspense/mystery
(a.k.a. Sherryl Woods, Suzanne Sherill)

**Kitt, Sandra** . . . . . . . . . . . . . . . category/ethnic

**Kitzmiller, Chelley** . . . . . . . . . . . . . . category

**Kleinsasser, Lois** . . . . . . . . . . . . . . . historical
(a.k.a. Cait London, Cait Logan)

**Koontz, Dean** . . . . . . . . . . . . . . . . . . category
(a.k.a. Leigh Kidder, Jane Nichols)

**Koppel, Lillian** (w/ Shelley Koppel) . . . category
(a.k.a. Lillian Shelley)

**Korbel, Kathleen** . . . . . . . . . . . . . . . . historical
(a.k.a. Eileen Dreyer)

**Krahn, Betina** . . . . . . . . . . . . . . . . . . category

**Krantz, Judith** . . . . . . . . . . . . . . contemporary

**Krentz, Jayne Ann** . . . . . category/mainstream/
(a.k.a. Jayne Taylor, Amanda Glass,    historical
Jayne Bentley, Jayne Castle,
Amanda Quick, Stephanie James)

**Kvokocz, Emily** . . . . . . . . . . . . . . . . . category
(a.k.a. Emily Carmichael, Emily Bradshaw)

**Kyle, Marlaine** . . . . . . . . . . . . . . . . . category
(a.k.a. Jean Hager, Leah Crane, Jeanne Stephens)

**Kyle, Susan** . . . . . . . . . . . . . .sci fi/contemprary
(a.k.a. Diana Blayne, Kate Curry, Diana Palmer)

**Ladd, Linda King** . . . . . . . . . . . . . . . . category
(a.k.a. Rita Clay Estrada)

**Lake, Rozella** . . . . . . . . . . . . . . . . . . category
(a.k.a. Roberta Leigh, Roumelia Lane,
Rachel Lindsay, Janet Scott)

**Lamb, Arnette** . . . . . . . . . . . . . . . . mainstream

**Lamb, Charlotte** . . . . . . . . . . category/historical
(a.k.a. Laura Hardy, Sheila Holland)

**Lambert, Willa** ................. category
(a.k.a. Bill Lambert)

**Landon, Nancy** ................. category
(a.k.a. Nancy Berland)

**Lane, Roumelia** ................ category
(a.k.a. Roberta Leigh, Rozella Lake,
Rachel Lindsay, Janey Scott)

**Lang, Eve** ..................... category
(a.k.a. Ruth Ryan Langan)

**Langan, Ruth Ryan** ............. category
(a.k.a. Eve Lang)

**Law, Rebecca Hagan** ............ category

**Lee, Elsie** ........ regency/romantic supense

**Lee, Linda** .................. contemporary
(a.k.a. Hope Goodwin, L. E. Bramwell)

**Lee, Rachel** .................... category
(a.k.a. Susan Civil)

**Leigh, Ana** .................... category
(a.k.a. Anna Lee Baier)

**Leigh, Jackie** .................. category
(a.k.a. Deborah Smith, Jacquelyn Lennox)

**Leigh, Petra** ................... category
(a.k.a. Peter Ling)

**Leigh, Roberta** ................ category
(a.k.a. Rozella Lake, Roumelia Lane,
Rachel Lindsay, Janey Scott)

**Leigh, Robin** .................. category
(a.k.a. Robin Lee Hatcher)

**Leigh, Tamara** ................. category

**Lemery, Alysse** ................ category
(a.k.a. Alysse Rasmussen)

**Lennox, Jacquelyn** ............. category
(a.k.a. Jackie Leigh, Deborah Smith)

**Lenore, Lisa** ................... category
(a.k.a. Craig Howard Broude)

**Leslie, Miriam** ................. category
(a.k.a. Dan Ross, W. E. Daniel Ross, Leslie Ames,
Ann Gilman, Ellen Randolph, Clarissa Ross,
Marilyn Ross, Jane Rossiter, Rose Williams)

**Leslie, Rochelle** ............... category
(a.k.a. Graham Diamond)

**Lester, Samantha** .............. category
(a.k.a. Lester Roper)

**Lewis, Debrah** . . . . . . . . . . . . . . . . . category
(a.k.a. James Conaway)

**Lind, Judi** . . . . . . . . . . . . . . . . . . . . category

**Lindsay, Rachel** . . . . . . . . . . . . . . . . . category
(a.k.a. Roberta Leigh, Rozella Lake,
Roumelia Lane, Janey Scott)

**Lindsey, Betina** . . . . . . . . . . . . . . . . . category

**Lindsey, Johanna** . . . . . . . . . . . . . . . historical

**Lindsey, Terri** . . . . . . . . . . . category/historical
(a.k.a. Terri Lynn, Terri Lynn Wilhelm)

**Ling, Peter** . . . . . . . . . . . . . . . . . . . category
(a.k.a. Petra Leigh)

**Link, Gail** . . . . . . . . . . . . . . . . . . . . category

**Linz, Cathie** . . . . . . . . . . . . . . . . . . historical
(a.k.a. Cathie Linz Baumgardner)

**Little, Paul** . . . . . . . . . . . . . . . . . . . category
(a.k.a. Paula Minton)

**Livingston, Georgette** . . . . . . . . . . . . category
(a.k.a. Camille Crawford, Diane Crawford)

**Lofts, Norah** . . . . . historical/romantic suspense
(a.k.a. Juliet Astley, Peter Curtis)

**Logan, Cait** . . . . . . . . . . . . . . . . . . . historical
(a.k.a. Cait London, Lois Kleinsasser)

**Logan, Daisy** . . . . . . . . . . . . category/historical
(a.k.a. Sara Orwig)

**Logan, Leandra** . . . . . . . . . . . . . . . . category
(a.k.a. Mary Schultz)

**Logan, Sara** . . . . . . . . . . . . . . . . . . . category
(a.k.a. June Hayden and Judith Simpson)

**London, Cait** . . . . . . . . . . . . . . . . . . historical
(a.k.a. Cait Logan, Lois Kleinsasser)

**London, Laura** . . . . . . . . . . . . . . . . . category
(a.k.a. Sharon and Tom Curtis, Robin James)

**Longrigg, Roger** . . . . . . . . . . . . . . . . category
(a.k.a. Megan Barker)

**Lord, Diana** . . . . . . . . . . . . . . . . . . mainstream
(a.k.a. Dawn Reno)

**Lorin, Amii** . . . . . . . . . . . . . . . . . . . category
(a.k.a. Joan Hohl, Paula Roberts)

**Lovelace, Merline** . . . . . . . . . . . . . . . category

**Lowell, Elizabeth** . . . . . . . . . . category/mystery
(a.k.a. Ann Maxwell,      contemporary/sci fi
A. E. Maxwell, Annalise Sun)

**Lowery, Marilyn M.** . . . . . . . . . . . . . . regency
(a.k.a. Philippa Castle)

**Lowry, Harold** . . . . . . . . . . . . . . . . . category
(a.k.a. Leigh Greenwood)

**Lynn, Terri** . . . . . . . . . . . . . category/historical
(a.k.a. Terri Lindsey, Terri Lynn Wilhelm)

**Lynson, Jane** . . . . . . . . . . . . . . . . . . category
(a.k.a. Lynn Michaels, Lynne A. Smith)

**Lyons, Leila** . . . . . . . . . . . . . . . . . category
(a.k.a. J. C. Conaway)

**Macaluso, Pamela** . . . . . . . . . . . . . . . . category

**Macias, Susan** . . . . . . . . . . . . . . . . category
(a.k.a. Susan Mallery)

**MacIver, Sharon** . . . . . . . . . . . . . . . . category
(a.k.a. Sharon Ihle, June Cameron)

**MacKeever, Maggie** . . . . . . . . . . . . . . . regency
(a.k.a. Gail Clark)

**Maclay, Charlotte** . . . . . . . . . . . . . . . . category
(a.k.a. Charlotte Lobb)

**MacLean, Anne** . . . . . . . . . . . . . . . . . category
(w/ Sandra Field)
(a.k.a. Jan MacLean, Jocelyn Haley)

**MacLean, Jan** . . . . . . . . . . . . . . . . . . category
(a.k.a. Anne MacLean and
Sandra Field, Jocelyn Haley)

**Macomber, Debbie** . . . . . . . . . . . . . . . category

**MacPherson, Selina** . . . . . . . . . . . . . historical
(a.k.a. Susan McClafferty)

**Madl, Linda** . . . . . . . . . . . . . . . . . . category

**Major, Ann** . . . . . . . . . . . . . . . . . . category
(a.k.a. Margaret Major Cleaves)

**Mallery, Susan** . . . . . . . . . . . . . . . . category
(a.k.a. Susan Macias)

**Mansfield, Elizabeth** . . . . . . . . . . . . . regency
(a.k.a. Paula Reibel Schwartz)

**Marchant, Catherine** . . . . category/mainstream
(a.k.a. Catherine Cookson, Katie McMullen)

**Martin, Deborah** . . . . . . . . . . . . . . . . category
(a.k.a. Deborah Nicholas)

**Martin, Kat** . . . . . . . . . . . . . . . . . . historical

**Mason, Connie** . . . . . . . . . . . . . . . . category
(a.k.a. Cara Miles)

**Mather, Anne** . . . . . . . . . . . . . . . . . category
(a.k.a. Mildred Greiveson)

| AUTHOR/pseudonyms | GENRE |
|---|---|

**Mathews, Pat** . . . . . . . . . . . . . . . . . . category
(w/ Denise Hrimak)
   (a.k.a. Denise Mathews)

**Matthews, Denise** . . . . . . . . . . . . . . category
   (a.k.a. Denise Hrimak and Pat Matthews)

**Matthews, Patricia & Clayton** . . . . . . historical

**Maxwell, Anne** . . . . contemporary/mystery/sci-fi
   (a.k.a. A. E. Maxwell, Elizabeth Lowell, Annalise Sun)

**Maxwell, Emily** . . . . . . . . . . . . . . . . . regency
   (a.k.a. Linda Schwab)

**Maxwell, Patricia** . . . . . . . . . . . . . . . . historical
   (a.k.a. Jennifer Blake)

**Maybury, Ann** . . . . . . . . . . . romantic suspense
   (a.k.a. Anne Buxton)

**Mayne, Elizabeth** . . . . . . . . . . . . . . . historical
   (a.k.a. Marietta Kaye Garcia)

**McBain, Laurie** . . . . . . . . . . . . . . . . . historical

**McBride, Mary** . . . . . . . . . . . . . . . . . . category
   (a.k.a. Mary Myers)

**McCaffrey, Anne** . . . . . . . . . . . . . . sci fi/fantasy

**McCall, Kathleen** . . . . . . . . . . . . . . . historical
   (a.k.a. Kathleen Drymon)

**McClafferty, Susan** . . . . . . . . . . . . . . historical
   (a.k.a. Selina McPherson)

**McComas, Mary Kay** . . . . . . . . . . . . . category

**McFather, Nelle** . . . . . . . . . . romantic suspense

**McKenna, Lindsay** . . . . . . . . . . . . . mainstream
   (a.k.a. Eileen Nauman, Beth Brookes)

**McKnight, Jenna** . . . . . . . . . . . . . . . . category
   (a.k.a. Ginny Schweiss)

**McMullen, Katie** . . . . . . . . category/mainstream
   (a.k.a. Catherine Cookson, Catherine Marchant)

**McNaught, Judith** . . . . . . . . . . . . . mainstream

**McPherren, Charlotte** . . . . . . . . . . . . category
   (a.k.a. Charla Chin and Jane Kidder, Charlotte Simms)

**McReynolds, Glenna** . . . . . . . . . . . . . category

**Meadowes, Alicia** . . . . . . . . . . . . . . . category
   (a.k.a. Linda Burak and Joan Zeig)

**Medeiros, Teresa** . . . . . . . . . . . . . . . . category

**Meinhardt, Shelly Thacker** . . . . . . . . historical
   (a.k.a. Shelly Thacker)

**Melville, Jennie** . . . . . . . . . . romantic suspense
   (a.k.a. Gwendoline Butler)

| AUTHOR/pseudonyms | GENRE |
|---|---|

**Morgan, Kathleen** ................ category
**Morsi, Pamela** ................. category
**Mortimer, Carol** ................ category
**Murphy, Lynne** .......... Native American
  (a.k.a. Georgina Gentry)
**Musgrave, David** ............... category
(w/ Jacqueline Musgrave)
  (a.k.a. Jacqueline Musgrave)
**Musgrave, Jacqueline** ............ category
  (a.k.a. Jacqueline and David Musgrave)
**Myers, Mary** ................... category
  (a.k.a. Mary McBride)
**Myers, Virginia** ................ category
(w/ Stella Cameron)
  (a.k.a. Jane Worth Abbott)
**Nauman, Eileen** ................ category
  (a.k.a. Lindsay McKenna, Beth Brookes)
**Neff, Linda** ................... category
**Neggers, Carla/Carla A.** ........... category/
  (a.k.a. Amalia James,       romantic suspense
  Anne Harrell)
**Nicholas, Deborah** .............. category
  (a.k.a. Deborah Martin)
**Nicholas, Robin** ............... category
  (a.k.a. Robin Kapala)
**Nichols, Leigh** ................ category
  (a.k.a. Dean Koontz)
**Nicole, Claudette** .............. category
  (a.k.a. Jon Messman)
**Norcross, Elisabet** ............. category
  (a.k.a. Arthur Gladstone, Margaret Sebastian)
**Nowasky, Jan** ................. historical
  (a.k.a. Lorraine Heath)
**O'Banyon, Constance** ........... historical
  (a.k.a. Evelyn Gee)
**O'Brien, Kathleen** .............. category
  (a.k.a. Kathleen Pynn)
**O'Day-Flannery, Constance** .......... category
**Ohlrogge, Anne Kristine Stuart** .... historical/
  (a.k.a. Anne Stuart)           gothic
**Oliver, Jan** ....................... category
  (a.k.a. Janece Oliver Hudson)
**Oliver, Patricia** ................. regency
  (a.k.a. Olivia Fontayne, Patricia De La Fuente)

**Orwig, Sara** . . . . . . . . . . . . .category/historical
(a.k.a. Daisy Logan)

**Osborne, Betsy** . . . . . . . . . . . . . contemporary
(a.k.a. Barbra Boswell)

**Osborne, Maggie** . . . . . . . . . . . . . . . historical
(a.k.a. Margaret St. George)

**Otten, Carol Card** . . . . . . . . . . . . . . . category
(w/ Ellen Lyle Taber)
(a.k.a. Tena Carlyle)

**Page, Betsy** . . . . . . . . . . . . . . . . . . . . category
(a.k.a. Elizabeth August,
Elizabeth Douglas, Bettie Marie Wilhite)

**Paige, Laurie** . . . . . . . . . . . . . . . . . . category
(a.k.a. Olivia M. Hall, Libby Hall)

**Pall, Ellen Jane** . . . . . . . . . . . . . . . . . regency
(a.k.a. Fiona Hill)

**Palmer, Diana** . . . . . . . . category/inspirational
(a.k.a. Diana Blayne, Kate Curry, Susan Kyle)

**Palmieri, Marina** . . . . . . . . . . . . . . . futuristic
(a.k.a. Marilyn Campbell)

**Paradise, Mary** . . . . . . . . . . . romantic suspense
(a.k.a. Dorothy Eden)

**Parker, Elizabeth** . . . . . . . . . . . . . . . . category

**Parmett, Doris** . . . . . . . . . . . . . . . . mainstream

**Parnell, Andrea** . . . . . . . . . . . . . . . . . category

**Patrick, DeAnn** . . . . . . . . . . . . . . . . . category
(a.k.a. Dotty Corcoran and Mary Ann Slojkowski)

**Pearl, Jack** . . . . . . . . . . . . . . . . . . . . . category
(a.k.a. Stephanie Blake)

**Peltonen, Carla** (w/ Molly Swanson) . . category
(a.k.a. Lynn Erickson)

**Pemberton, Nan** . . . . . . . . . . . . . . . . category
(a.k.a. Ann Coombs, Nina Coombs, Nina Porter,
Nora Powers, Nina Pykare, Regina Towers)

**Peters, Anne** . . . . . . . . . . . . . . . . . . . category
(a.k.a. Annegret Hansen)

**Peters, Elizabeth** . . . . . . . . . romantic suspense
(a.k.a. Barbara Michaels)

**Phillips, Dorothy** . . . . . . . . . . . . . . . . category
(a.k.a. Dorothy Garlock,
Dorothy Glenn, Joanna Phillips)

**Phillips, Joanna** . . . . . . . . . . . . . . . . . category
(a.k.a. Dorothy Phillips,
Dorothy Garlock, Dorothy Glenn)

**Phillips, Susan** . . . . . . . . . . . . . . . . . category
(w/ Claire Kiehl)
   (a.k.a. Justine Cane)

**Pickart, June Elliott** . . . . . . . . . . . . . . category
   (a.k.a. Robin Elliott)

**Pilcher, Rosamund** . . . . . . . . . . . . mainstream
   (a.k.a. Jane Fraser)

**Plaidy, Jean** . . . . . . . . . . . . . . . . . . . historical
   (a.k.a. Eleanor Burford Hibbert,
   Victoria Holt, Philippa Carr)

**Poole, Rhoda Janssen** . . . . . . . . . . . . category
   (a.k.a. Krista Janssen)

**Porter, Madeline and**
**Harper, Shannon** . . . . . . . . . . . . . . . category/
   (a.k.a. Elizabeth Habersham,     historical
   Madeline Harper, Anna James)

**Porter, Nina** . . . . . . . . . . category/contemporary
   (a.k.a. Ann Coombs, Nina Coombs, Nan Pemberton,
   Nora Powers, Nina Pykare, Regina Towers)

**Potter, Patricia** . . . . . . . . . . . . . . . . . historical

**Powell, Cynthia** . . . . . . . . . . . . . contemporary

**Power, JoAnn and**
**Cummings, Barbara** . . . . mainstream/category
   (a.k.a. Ann Crowleigh)

**Powers, Nora** . . . . . . . . category/contemporary
   (a.k.a. Ann Coombs, Nina Coombs, Nan Pemberton,
   Nina Pykare, Regina Towers)

**Pozzessere, Heather Graham** . . . . . . . . historical
   (a.k.a. Heather Graham, Shannon Drake)

**Prestie, Taylor Caldwell** . . . . . . . . . . historical
   (a.k.a. Taylor Caldwell)

**Preston, Fayrene** . . . . . . . . . . . . . . . . category
   (a.k.a. Jaelyn Conlee)

**Price, Ashland** . . . . . . . . . . . . . . . . . category
   (a.k.a. Janice Carlson)

**Pryor, Pauline** . . . . . . . . . . . . . . . . . . category
   (a.k.a. Elisabeth Welles, Mary Wilson,
   Mary Linn Roby, Valerie Bradshaw,
   Pamela D'Arcy, Georgina Grey)

**Pykare, Nina** . . . . . . . . . . . . . . . contemporary
   (a.k.a. Nina Coombs, Ann Coombs, Nan Pemberton,
   Nina Porter, Nora Powers, Regina Towers)

**Pynn, Kathleen** . . . . . . . . . . . . . . . . . category
   (a.k.a. Kathleen O'Brien)

**Quick, Amanda** . . . . . . . . . . . . . . . . . historical
(a.k.a. Jayne Ann Krentz, Jayne Bentley,
Jayne Castle, Amanda Glass, Stephanie James)

**Quinn, Tara Taylor** . . . . . . . . . . . . . . category

**Quinto, Carol** . . . . . . . . . . . . . . . . . . regency
(a.k.a. Jeanne Carmichael, Carol Michaels)

**Radcliffe, Janette** . . . . . . . . . . .regency/category
(a.k.a. Janet Louise Roberts,
Rebecca Danton, Louisa Bronte)

**Rampling, Anne** . . . . . . .vampire/erotica/sensual
(a.k.a. Anne Rice, A. N. Roquelaure)

**Randall, Diana** . . . . . . . . . . . . . . . . . category
(a.k.a. Dan Ross, W. E. Daniel Ross,
Ellen Randolph, Leslie Ames, Marilyn Carter,
Clarissa Ross, Marilyn Ross, Jane Rossiter,
Rose Williams, Ann Gilmer, Miriam Leslie)

**Randolph, Ellen** . . . . . . . . . . . . . . . . . category
(a.k.a. Diana Randall, Dan Ross,
W. E. Daniel Ross, Leslie Ames,
Marilyn Carter, Ellen Randolph,
Clarissa Ross, Marilyn Ross, Jane Rossiter,
Rose Williams, Ann Gilmer, Miriam Leslie)

**Ransom, Diana** . . . . . . . category/contemporary
(a.k.a. Nancy Gideon, Lauren Giddings)

**Rasley, Alicia** . . . . . . . . . . . . . . . . . . . . category
(a.k.a. Elisabeth Todd, Michelle Venet)

**Rasmussen, Alysse** . . . . . . . . . . . . contemporary
(a.k.a. Alysse Lemery)

**Rawlings, Louisa** . . . . . . . . . . . . . . . . category
(a.k.a. Sylvia Baumgarten, Sylvia Halliday)

**Redd, Joanna** . . . . . . . . . . . . . . . . . . historical
(a.k.a. Lauren Wilde)

**Reife, Alan** . . . . . . . . . . . . . . . . . . . . category
(a.k.a. Barbara Reife)

**Reife, Barbara** . . . . . . . . . . . . . . . . . . category
(a.k.a. Alan Reife)

**Reisser, Anne** . . . . . . . . . . . . . . . . . . . category

**Reno, Dawn** . . . . . . . . . . . . . . . . mainstream
(a.k.a. Diana Lord)

**Reynard, Carol** . . . . . . . . . . . . . . . . . . category
(a.k.a. Shirl Henke)

**Rice, Anne** . . . . . . . . . . . vampire/erotica/sensual
(a.k.a. A. N. Roquelaure, Anne Rampling)

**Rice, Patricia** . . . . . . . . . . . . . . . . . . category

| AUTHOR/pseudonyms | GENRE |
|---|---|

**Rieger, Catherine** . . . . . . . . . . . . . . . . category
**Riker, Leigh** . . . . . . . . . . . . . . . . . . category
**Rinehold, Connie** . . . . . . . . . . . . . . . category
**Robarchek, Peg** . . . . . . . . . . . . . . . category
(a.k.a. Peg Sutherland)
**Robb, JoAnn** . . . . . . . . . . . . . . . . . category
(a.k.a. JoAnn Ross, JoAnn Robbins)
**Robbins, Kay** . . . . . . . . . . . . . . . . . category
(a.k.a. Kay Hooper)
**Roberts, Janet Louise** . . . . . . . . . . . . regency
(a.k.a. Janette Radcliffe,
Rebecca Danton, Louisa Brönte)
**Roberts, Kelsey** . . . . . . . . . . . . . . . category
(a.k.a. Rhonda Harding-Pollero)
**Roberts, Nora** . . . . . . . . . . category/mainstream
**Robins, Gina** . . . . . . . . . . . . . . . . . category
(a.k.a. Carol Finch, Connie Fedderson,
Connie Drake)
**Robbins, Kay** . . . . . . . . . . . . .category/futuristic
(a.k.a. Kay Hooper)
**Roby, Mary Linn** . . . . . . . . . . regency/category
(a.k.a. Valerie Bradshaw, Pamela D'Arcy, Georgina
Grey, Pauline Pryor, Elisabeth Welles, Mary Wilson)
**Rogers, Evelyn and
Davenport, Kathryn** . . . . . . . . . . . . . category
(a.k.a. Keller Graves)
**Rogers, Marylyle** . . . . . . . . . . . . . . . category
**Rogers, Rosemary** . . . . . . . . . . . . . . historical
**Rome, Elaine** . . . . . . . . . . . . . . . . . historical
(a.k.a. Elaine Barbieri)
**Roper, Lester** . . . . . . . . . . . . . . . . category
(a.k.a. Samantha Lester)
**Roquelaure, A. N.** . . . . .vampire/erotica/sensual
(a.k.a. Anne Rice, Anne Rampling)
**Ross, Clarissa** . . . . . . . . . . . . . . . . . category
(a.k.a. Dan Ross, W. E. Daniel Ross,
Leslie Ames, Marilyn Carter, Ann Gilmer,
Miriam Leslie, Diana Randall, Ellen Randolph,
Marilyn Ross, Jane Rossiter, Rose Williams)
**Ross, Dan** . . . . . . . . . . . . . . . . . . . category
(a.k.a. Clarissa Ross, W. E. Daniel Ross,
Leslie Ames, Marilyn Carter, Ann Gilmer,
Miriam Leslie, Diana Randall, Ellen Randolph,
Marilyn Ross, Jane Rossiter, Rose Williams)

**Ross, W. E. Daniel** . . . . . . . . . . . . . . . category
  (a.k.a. Leslie Ames, Marilyn Carter,
  Ann Gilmer, Miriam Leslie, Diana Randall,
  Ellen Randolph, Clarissa Ross, Dan Ross,
  Marilyn Ross, Jane Rossiter, Rose Williams)
**Ross, Marilyn** (see Dan Ross) . . . . . . . . category
**Ross, JoAnn** . . . . . . . . . . . . . . . . . . . . category
  (a.k.a. JoAnn Robb, JoAnn Robbins)
**Rossiter, Jane** (see Dan Ross) . . . . . . . . category
**Rothman, Marcy Elias** . . . . . . . . . . . . category
**Royall, Vanessa** . . . . . . . . . . . . . . . . . historical
  (a.k.a. Mike Hinkemeyer)
**Ryan, Nan** . . . . . . . . . . . . . . . . . . . . . historical
**Ryan, Rachel** . . . . . . . . . . . category/mainstream
  (a.k.a. Laura Jordan, Erin St. Clair, Sandra Brown)
**St. Clair, Erin** . . . . . . . . . . category/mainstream
  (a.k.a. Sandra Brown, Laura Jordan, Rachel Ryan)
**St. Clair, Stephanie** . . . . . . . . . . . . . . category
  (a.k.a. Donald Maas)
**St. George, Margaret** . . . . . . . . . . . . . category
  (a.k.a. Maggie Osborne)
**Sager, Esther** . . . . . . . . . . . . . . . contemporary
**Sala, Sharon** . . . . . . . . . . . . . . . . . . . category
**Salvato, Sharon** . . . . . . . . . . . . . . . . . category
(w/ Cornelia Parkinson)
  (a.k.a. Day Taylor)
**Sanders, Glenda** . . . . . . . . . . category/historcal
  (a.k.a. Glenda Sands, Glenda Kachelmeier)
**Sanders, Lisa** . . . . . . . . . . . . . . . category/ethnic
  (a.k.a. Angela and Sandra Jackson)
**Sands, Glenda** . . . . . . . . . . . . category/historical
  (a.k.a. Glenda Kachelmeier, Glenda Sanders)
**Santori, Helen** . . . . . young adult/contemporary
  (a.k.a. Helen Erskine)
**Sattler, Veronica** . . . . . . . . . . . . . . . . category
**Saunders, Diana** . . . . . . . . . . . . category/gothic
  (a.k.a. Virginia Edith Coffman, Victor Cross,
  Virginia Deuval, Jeanne Duval, Ann Standfield)
**Sawyer, John** . . . . . . . . . . . . . . . . . . . category
(w/ Nancy Buckingham)
  (a.k.a. Nancy John)
**Sawyer, Meryl** . . . . . . . . . . . . . . . . . . category
  (a.k.a. Martha Unickel, Meryl Nickles)

| AUTHOR/pseudonyms | GENRE |
|---|---|

**Saxe, Coral Smith** . . . . . . . . . . . . . . . . category
**Schaal, Elizabeth** . . . . . . . . . . . . . . . category
(w/ Elaine Cichanth)
    (a.k.a. Elizabeth Shelley)
**Schere, Monroe and Jean** . . . . . . . . . . category
    (a.k.a. Jessica Howard)
**Schimek, Gayle Malone** . . . . . . . contemporary
    (a.k.a. Joleen Daniels)
**Schwab, Linda** . . . . . . . . . . . . . . . . . . . regency
    (a.k.a. Emily Maxwell)
**Schweiss, Ginny** . . . . . . . . . . . . . . . . category
    (a.k.a. Jenny McKnight)
**Schwartz, Paula Reibel** . . . . . . . . . . . . regency
    (a.k.a. Elizabeth Mansfield)
**Schultz, Mary** . . . . . . . . . . . . . . . . . . . category
    (a.k.a. Leandra Logan)
**Scofield, Lee** . . . . . . . . . . . . . . . . . . . category
**Scott, Deloras** . . . . . . . . . . . . . . . . . . category
**Scott, Janey** . . . . . . . . . . . . . . . . . . . . category
    (a.k.a. Roberta Leigh, Rozella Lake,
    Roumelia Lane, Rachel Lindsay)
**Scott, Susan Holloway** . . . . . . . . . . . . historical
    (a.k.a. Miranda Jarrett)
**Scott, Theresa** . . . . . . . . . . . . . . . . . . category
**Sebastian, Margaret** . . . . . . . . . . . . . . category
    (a.k.a. Elisabet Norcross, Arthur Gladstone)
**Seidick, Kathryn** . . . . . . . . . . . . . . . . category
    (a.k.a. Michelle Kasey, Kasey Michaels)
**Seton, Anya** . . . . . . . . . . . . . . . . . . . historical
**Shayne, Maggie** . . . . . . . . . . . . . . . . category
    (a.k.a. Margaret Benson)
**Shaw, Linda** . . . . . . . . . . . . . . . . . . . . category
**Shelley, Elizabeth** . . . . . . . . . . . . . . . category
    (a.k.a. Elizabeth Schaal and Elaine Cichanth)
**Shelley, Lillian** . . . . . . . . . . . . . . . . . category
    (a.k.a. Lillian and Shelley Koppel)
**Sherill, Suzanne** . . . . . . . . . . . suspense/mystery
    (a.k.a. Sherryl Woods, Alexandra Kirk)
**Sherwood, Valerie** . . . . . . . . . . . . . . . historical
    (a.k.a. Jeanne Hines)
**Shiplett, June Lund** . . . . . . . . . . . . time travel
**Siegenthal, Deb** . . . . . . . . . . . . . . . . historical
    (a.k.a. Deborah Simmons)

**Simas, Ann** . . . . . . . . . . . . . . . . . . . . category
(a.k.a. Annie Sims)

**Simon, Joann** . . . . . . . . . . . . . . . . . . time travel

**Simmons, Deborah** . . . . . . . . . . . . . . historical
(a.k.a. Deb Siegenthal)

**Simms, Charlotte** . . . . . . . . . . . . . . . . category
(a.k.a. Charlotte McPherren,
Charla Chin and Jane Kidder)

**Simms, Suzanne** . . . . . . . . . . . . . . . . . category
(a.k.a. Suzanne Simmons Guntrum)

**Simpson, Judith** . . . . . . . . . . . . . . . . . category
(w/ June Hayden)
(a.k.a. Sara Logan, Rosalind Foxx)

**Sims, Annie** . . . . . . . . . . . . . . . . . . . . . category
(a.k.a. Ann Simas)

**Sinclair, Elizabeth** . . . . . . . . . . . . . . . category
(a.k.a. Marguerite Smith)

**Sizemore, Susan** . . . . . . . . . . . . . . . . . category

**Sizer, Mona** . . . . . . . . . . . . . . . . . . . . . category
(a.k.a. Deana James)

**Skinner, Gloria Dale** . . . . . . . . . . . . . category
(a.k.a. Charla Cameron)

**Skye, Christina** . . . . . . . . . . . . . . . . . . category
(a.k.a. Roberta Helmer)

**Small, Bertrice** . . . . . . . . . . . . . . . . . historical

**Smith, Alana** . . . . . . . . . . . . . . . . . . . . category
(a.k.a. Bruce Smith)

**Smith, Bobbi** . . . . . . . . . . . . . . . . . . . . category

**Smith, Bruce** . . . . . . . . . . . . . . . . . . . . category
(a.k.a. Alana Smith)

**Smith, Dana Warren** . . . . . . . . . . . . . category
(a.k.a. Lisa G. Brown)

**Smith, Deborah** . . . . . . . . . . . . . . . . . category
(a.k.a. Jackie Leigh, Jacquelyn Lennox)

**Smith, Debra** . . . . . . . . . . . . . . . . . . historical

**Smith, Joan** . . . . . . . . . . . . . . . . . . . . . regency
(a.k.a. Jennie Gallant)

**Smith, Karen Rose** . . . . . . . . . . . . . . . category
(a.k.a. Kari Sutherland)

**Smith, Marguerite** . . . . . . . . . . . . . . . category
(a.k.a. Elizabeth Sinclair)

**Snoe, Eboni** . . . . . . . . . . . . . . . category/ethnic

**Stables, Mira** . . . . . . . . . . . . . . . . . . . . regency

**Stadler, Jill** . . . . . . . . . . . . . . . . . . . . historical
(a.k.a. Jill Barnett)

**Standfield, Ann** . . . . . . . . . . . . . category/gothic
(a.k.a. Virginia Edith Coffman, Victor Cross,
Virginia Deuval, Jeanne Duval, Diana Saunders)

**Steel, Danielle** . . . . . contemporary/mainstream

**Stephens, Jeanne** . . . .category/Native American
(a.k.a. Leah Crane, Jean Hager, Marlaine Kyle)

**Stewart, Mary** . . . . .historical/romantic suspense

**Stockenberg, Antoinette** . . . . . . . . . . category
(a.k.a. Suzanne Hoos)

**Stuart, Anne** . . . . . . . . . . . . . . historical/gothic
(a.k.a. Anne Kristine Stuart Ohlrogge)

**Stuart, Elizabeth** . . . . . . . . . . . . . . . . category

**Summers, Essie** . . . . . . . . . . . . . . . . category

**Summerville, Margaret** . . . . . . . . . . . category
(a.k.a. Barbara and Pamela Wilson)

**Sun, Annalise** . . . . . . . . . . . . . . . . . . . category
(a.k.a. A. E. Maxwell,          contemporary/sci fi
Ann Maxwell, Elizabeth Lowell)

**Suson, Marlene** . . . . . . . . . . . . . . . . . . category

**Sutherland, Kari** . . . . . . . . . . . . . . . . category
(a.k.a. Karen Rose Smith)

**Sutherland, Peg** . . . . . . . . . . . . . . . . category
(a.k.a. Peg Robarchek)

**Swanson, Molly** (w/ Carla Peltonen) . . category
(a.k.a. Lynn Erickson)

**Swift, Linda** . . . . . . . . . . . . . . . . . . . . category

**Taber, Ellen Lyle** . . . . . . . . . . . . . . . . category
(w/ Carol Card Otlen)
(a.k.a. Tena Carlyle)

**Taylor, Day** . . . . . . . . . . . . . . . . . . . . category
(a.k.a. Sharon Salvato and Cornelia Parkinson)

**Taylor, Janelle** . . . . . . . . . . . . . . . . . historical

**Taylor, Jayne** . . . . . . . . . . . . . . . contemporary
(a.k.a. Jayne Ann Krentz, Jayne Bentley,
Amanda Glass, Amanda Quick, Jayne Castle,
Stephanie James)

**Thacker, Shelly** . . . . . . . . . . . . . . . . . historical
(a.k.a. Shelly Thacker Meinhardt)

**Thayer, Patricia** . . . . . . . . . . . . . . . . category
(a.k.a. Patricia Wright)

**Theis, Joyce** (w/ Janet Bieber) . . . . . . . category
(a.k.a. Janet Joyce)

**Thurlow, Kathy** . . . . . . . . . . . . . . . . category
**Titchenor, Louise** . . . . . . . . . . . . . . category
   (a.k.a. Ruth Glick, Alyssa Howard,
   Eileen Bucholtz, Alexis Hill Jordan)
**Todd, Elizabeth** . . . . . . . . . . . . . contemporary
   (a.k.a. Alicia Ramsley, Michelle Venet)
**Toombs, John** . . . . . . . . . . . . . . . . . . . category
   (a.k.a. Fortune Kent, Jocelyn Wilde)
**Toothman, Catherine Ann** . . . . . . . . . . category
   (a.k.a. Cathleen Clare)
**Towers, Regina** . . . . . . . category/contemporary
   (a.k.a. Ann Coombs, Nina Coombs, Nina Porter,
   Nan Pemberton, Nora Powers, Nina Pykare)
**Torday, Ursula** . . . . . . . . . . . . . . . . . . regency
   (a.k.a. Paula Allardyce)
**Tracy, Marie** . . . . . . . . . . . . . . . . . . . . category
   (a.k.a. Audra Adams)
**Tremaine, Jennie** . . . . . . . . . . category/regency
   (a.k.a. Marion Chesney, Marion
   Chesney Gibbons, Helen Crampton, Ann Fairfax)
**Trent, Lynda** . . . . . . . . . . . . . . . . . . . . category
   (a.k.a. Lynda and Dan Trent)
**Unickel, Martha** . . . . . . . . . . . . . . . . . category
   (a.k.a. Meryl Nickles, Meryl Sawyer)
**Vale Allen, Charlotte** . . . . . . . . . . contemporary
**Valentine, Donna** . . . . . . . . . . . . . . . . category
**Van Slyke, Helen** . . . . . . . . . . . . . mainstream
   (a.k.a. Sharon Aston)
**Vaughan, Vivian** . . . . . . . . . . . . . . . . . category
**Vayle, Valerie** . . . . . . . . . . . . . . . . . . . category
   (a.k.a. Janice Young Brooks and
   Jean Brooks-Janowiak)
**Venet, Michelle** . . . . . . . . . . . . . . . . . category
   (a.k.a. Alicia Rasley, Elizabeth Todd)
**Verge, Vivian** . . . . . . . . . . . . . . . . . . . category
**Veryan, Patricia** . . . . . . . . . . . . . . . . . regency
   (a.k.a. Patricia Bannister)
**Vest, Jo Ann** . . . . . . . . . . . . . . . . . . . category
   (a.k.a. Joanna Wayne)
**Vitek, Donna** . . . . . . . . . . . . . . . . . . . category
   (a.k.a. Donna Alexander)
**Wagner, Carol I.** . . . . . . . . . . . . . . . . . category
(w/ JoAnne Bremer)
   (a.k.a. Joellyn Carroll)

| AUTHOR/pseudonyms | GENRE |
|---|---|

**Walker, Laurie** . . . . . . . . . . . . . . . . . category
(a.k.a. G. Laurie Gilbert)

**Walsh, Sheila** . . . . . . . . . . . . . . . . . regency

**Ward, Lynda** . . . . . . . . .regency/contemporary
(a.k.a. Julia Jeffries)

**Ware, Ciji** . . . . . . . . . . . . . . . . . . . category

**Washington, Elsie** . . . . . . . . . . . category/ethnic
(a.k.a. Rosalind Welles)

**Watson, Julia** . . . . . . . . . . . . . . . . . historical
(a.k.a. Julia Fitzgerald, Joanna Wayne)

**Wayne, Joanna** . . . . . . . . . . . . . . . . . category
(a.k.a. Jo Ann Vest, Julia Watson)

**Webb, Peggy** . . . . . . . . . . . . . . . . . category

**Weger, Jackie** . . . . . . . . . . . . . . category/ethnic

**Weir, Theresa** . . . . . . . . . . . . . . . . . fantasy

**Weldon, Susan** . . . . . . . . . . . . . . . . . historical

**Welles, Rosalind** . . . . . . . . . . . category/ethnic
(a.k.a. Elsie Washington)

**West, Chassie** . . . . . . . . . . . . . category/ethnic
(a.k.a. Tracy West)

**West, Tracy** . . . . . . . . . . . . . . category/ethnic
(a.k.a. Chassie West)

**Weyrich, Becky Lee** . . . . . . category/time travel

**Whitmer-Gow, Karyn** . . . . . . . . . . . . category
(a.k.a. Elizabeth Kary)

**Whitney, Phyllis A.** . . . . . . . . romantic suspense

**Wide, Jocelyn** . . . . . . . . . . . . . . . . . category
(a.k.a. John Toombs)

**Wie, Pat Van** . . . . . . . . . . . . . . . . . category
(a.k.a. Patricia Keelyn)

**Wiete, Robin Lee** . . . . . . . . . . . . . . . category
(a.k.a. Leanne Grayson)

**Wiggs, Susan** . . . . . . . . . . . . . . . . . historical
(a.k.a. Susan Childress)

**Wilde, Jennifer** . . . . . . . . . . . . . . . . historical
(a.k.a. Tom E. Huff)

**Wilde, Lauren** . . . . . . . . . . . . . . . . . category
(a.k.a. Joanna Redd)

**Wilhelm, Terri Lynn** . . . . . . . . . . . . . category/
(a.k.a. Terri Lynn, Terri Lindsey)     historical

**Wilhite, Bettie Marie** . . . . . . . . . . . . . category
(a.k.a. Elizabeth August,
Elizabeth Douglas, Betsy Page)

**Wilkins, Margaret** . . . . . . . . . . . . . . . . category
(a.k.a. Margaret Moore)

**Wilkinson, Cherry** . . . . . . . . . . . . . . . category
(a.k.a. Cherry Adair)

**Williams, Rose** . . . . . . . . . . . . . . . . . . category
(a.k.a. Dan Ross, W. E. Daniel Ross,
Leslie Ames, Marilyn Carter, Ann Gilmer,
Miriam Leslie, Diana Randall, Ellen Randolph,
Clarissa Ross, Marilyn Ross, Jane Rossiter)

**Willman, Marianne** . . . . . . . . . . . . . . category
(a.k.a. Marianne Clark, Sabina Clark)

**Wilson, Barbara and Pamela** . . . . . . . . category
(a.k.a. Margaret Summerville)

**Winberly, Clara** . . . . . . . . . . . . . . . . . category

**Wind, David** . . . . . . . . . . . . . . . . . . . . category
(a.k.a. Monica Barrie, Jenifer Dalton, Gena Dalton)

**Windsor, Linda** . . . . . . . . . . . . . . . . . . category
(a.k.a. Linda Covington)

**Winsor, Kathleen** . . . . . . . . . . . . . . . . historical

**Winspear, Violet** . . . . . . . . . . . . . . . . . category

**Wolf, Joan** . . . . . . . . . . . . . . . . . . . . . . regency

**Wood, Deborah** . . . . . . . . . . . . . . . . . historical
(a.k.a. Debbi Wood)

**Woodiwiss, Kathleen** . . . . . . . . . . . . . historical

**Woods, Sherryl** . . . . . . . . . . . suspense/mystery
(a.k.a. Alexandra Kirk, Suzanne Sherill)

**Wright, Cynthia** . . . . . . . . . . . . . . . . historical
(a.k.a. Cynthia Wright Hunt)

**Wright, Patricia** . . . . . . . . . . . . . . . . . category
(a.k.a. Patricia Thacker)

**Wulf, Jessica** . . . . . . . . . . . . . . . . . . . category

**Yansick, Susan** . . . . . . . . . . . . . . . . . . category
(w/ Christine Healy)
(a.k.a. Erin Yorke)

**Yirka, Barbara** . . . . . . . . . . . . . . . . . . category
(a.k.a. Anne Barbour)

# $\mathcal{H}$OW TO THINK AND TALK LIKE A ROMANCE COLLECTOR

## CHAPTER 3

You will need to be aware of the following areas to become a collector of romance novels.

## TODAY'S MARKET TRENDS

Book searchers have recognized that some authors are more popular in certain parts of the country than in others. For instance, Linda Lael Miller, Laura Parker, Nan Ryan, Brenda Joyce, and Iris Johansen are popular in Eastern states, while Southern readers prefer Essie Summers and Betty Neels. Western readers search for books by such authors as Ann Maxwell, Georgina Gentry, Joan Hohl and Debbie Macomber. Midwest readers like Cassie Edwards, Susan Johnson and Joan Johnston. Collectors all over the country are looking for books by Jayne Ann Krentz, Stephanie James, Linda Howard, Sandra Brown, Elizabeth Lowell, Diana Palmer, Kay Hooper, and Nora Roberts.

The Network has noticed that reading and collecting trends seem to coincide with new releases and book reviews by *Romantic Times*. Bookstore clerks also have a lot of influence when it comes to promoting an author—if they tell their customers about a book, it not only helps the customer but the author as well.

*Two novels by Essie Summers, including a collection of three of her works (printed by Harlequin Omnibus 36) and* Sweet Are the Ways *(Harlequin Romance, #1015). Courtesy of Jacque Tiegs.*

*Jayne Ann Krentz's* Ghost of a Chance *(Harlequin Temptation, #34). From the collection of Peg Reno.*

*Susan Johnson's* Golden Paradise *(Harlequin Historical, #51). Courtesy of Jacque Tiegs.*

*Three novels by Brenda Joyce:* Innocent Fire *(Avon),* Violet Fire *(Avon) and* Firestorm *(Avon). Courtesy of Jacque Tiegs.*

*Sandra Brown's*
Thursday's Child
*(Loveswept, #79).*
Courtesy of Jacque Tiegs.

*Group of Kay Hooper's novels:* Summer of the Unicorn
*(Bantam),* Raven on the Wing *(Loveswept, #193),* House
of Cards: *A Lane Montana Mystery (Avon),* Crime of
Passion *(Avon), and* If There Be Dragons *(Loveswept,
#71).* Courtesy of Jacque Tiegs.

*Group of Jayne Castle's novels (Guinevere Jones titles):* The
Desperate Game, The Chilling Deception, The Sinister
Touch, and The Fatal Fortune. *All published by Dell.*
Courtesy of Jacque Tiegs.

But, as with other commodities, supply and demand is what controls the market. For example, when a popular author writes under a pseudonym, the a.k.a name often goes unnoticed; this was the case with the MacFadden books written by Jayne Castle and Jayne Bentley. Although a lot of readers kept the Castle books, knowing they were written by popular author Jayne Ann Krentz, almost all threw away the Jayne Bentley books, not realizing they were also written by Krentz. To confuse the matter further, Krentz has written immensely popular historical novels under the name Amanda Quick; she has also used other pseudonyms including Stephanie James, Amanda Glass, and Jayne Taylor. Once collectors discovered the MacFadden books, the price of the ones written by Krentz skyrocketed in value because there were so few on the market since the MacFaddens are no longer being printed.

Bookstores which specialize in used books rarely see new books for at least three to six months after their release. Those bookstores also have the same lack of space that "new" bookstores do. Thus, trends may often be created simply because bookstore owners throw out older, $2.00 and under, slow-moving books, to make room for more expensive ($3.95–$6.00), better-looking (and selling) recent ones. As a result, for instance, some of the earlier Harlequins (e.g., the medical profession or nurse series) are few and far between. Although there may be collectors searching for such books, they will rarely find them in bookstores. When they do, the books will be sold for extremely reasonable prices because there is little demand for them in the market.

Even though it is difficult to predict what will be popular in the future, a collector can never go wrong keeping books that are interesting to that person, ones by popular authors (whether written under a pseudonym or not), autographed books, or a line of books which is no longer being published (i.e. Kismet/Meteor, which recently went out of business after making a splash in the romance world).

*Marguerite Mooers Marshall's* Wilderness Nurse *(Pocket).*
Courtesy of Jacque Tiegs.

We believe the fairly new multi-cultural or ethnic romances are going to be very hot. If you are there at the beginning of a trend, it is always wise to pick up first edition copies and, if possible, to get them signed by the author. Writers like Sandra Kitt and Eboni Snoe are fairly accessible, have appeared at conferences like those held by *Romantic Times*, and can be reached through their publishers. It is interesting that a recent issue of one of the bookstore newspapers featured ethnic romances in the section where new titles are promoted. Editors and readers alike are excited about the new avenues these books will open. We suggest you keep apprised of the new novels that become available in this area of romance fiction.

In the same way, Native American books are enjoying a resurgence in popularity. It seems public interest in Southwestern and Native American art and decoration has trickled down into the romance book field. Authors Janelle Taylor and Georgina Gentry, for example, have made their romances about Native Americans especially enjoyable because they've spent so much time and energy researching their subjects and paying attention to detail. When a topic is hot, as Native American romance is, the collector should be aware of that fact and pick up numerous copies of the book. The only "drawback," if you could call it that, is most Native American romances are not considered category books—in other words, they are large books with fairly substantial print runs. These authors have enormous followings thus their books are easy to find. Remember, it's the hard-to-find books that become the most valuable!

A brief word on autographed books. An autograph automatically doubles the value of the book. If you get a book which is autographed, take special care not to bend or crack the binding. If the book remains in mint condition, the autograph will often triple the book's market value. It can sometimes make the book invaluable if, for example, the author had rarely done a signing. This is the case with Linda Howard, an author who, because she developed tendonitis, used a stamp to sign her books. If one were to find an actual handwritten Linda Howard autograph, therefore, the book would be worth much more than the stamped version.

Some author's autographs that have become collectible include: Jean Auel ($5–$25), Jane Austen ($700–$5,000), Taylor Caldwell ($30–$175), Barbara Cartland ($20–$80), Janet Dailey ($5–$10), Grace Livingston Hill ($25–$80), and Margaret Mitchell ($500–$2,500). These prices reflect autographs only and do not include the value of the book itself. (We refer you to *The Price Guide to Autographs*, (George Sanders, Helen Sanders and Ralph Roberts) Wallace-Homestead Book Co., Radnor, Penn., 1991.)

If you are collecting a favorite author's autograph, keep in mind that these writers often send promotional materials about their next book to their fans. Bookmarks, pencils, greeting cards, press releases, photographs, and book covers are just some of the giveaways you can collect (for free!) at conferences, book signings, and conventions. Arrange to get your name on your favorite author's mailing list and soon you will have an abundance of signed collectibles and other trinkets to add to your romance memorabilia.

Recently, many collectors have shown interest in certain books strictly because of the book's cover art, a situation that irritates writers immensely. For example, since the cover model Fabio has become a superstar, the early books for which he modelled (especially those where his normally blonde hair is dark) are considered collectible. Steve Sandalis, "The Topaz Man," is also a celebrity of sorts. This was evident by the crowds he attracted at the last *Romantic Times* convention. The Bartling Brothers, a trio of blond, beautiful and brawny Nebraskan brothers who formerly were pig farmers, are also becoming well known.

One little-known secret in the market is that superstar Tom Selleck began his career as a model on romance covers. We are willing to bet if you can find the books for which he modelled, they will be worth much more than their original cover price.

Some final words of advice about market trends. Watch the rising stars in the romance world, never miss the opportunity to meet your favorite authors at book signings or conventions and conferences (these are held almost every weekend at various locations across the country), hold on to your auto-graphed copies, and keep searching for books by your favorite authors. Use the resources outlined in this book to keep in touch with other readers and collectors, authors, and publishers. There are thousands of people who share your interests. By developing a relationship with them, you are widening your network and increasing your chances of adding those special favorites to your collection. Remember bookstore owners, authors, and publishers are people, too. They love to hear about your favorite books and authors. And who knows, by contacting an author, you might even receive a signed book, bookmark or special promo-tional item to add to your collection!

## HOW TO ASSESS A BOOK'S CONDITION

As you collect, you will find that the condition of your romance novels will be of paramount impor-tance. No one wants to add an abused book to their collection but, if you find an exceptionally rare example, you may be forced to lower your stan-dards occasionally. Thus, it is important for us to define the standards booksellers and searchers use when they ascertain the condition of paperback books. Because most romances are published in paperback, we will not discuss hardcovers here. However, we are aware that this trend is changing and that we will begin to see more romance authors published in hardcover.

| CONDITION | DESCRIPTION |
|---|---|
| Mint/A | The spine of the book is unbroken; pages are not bent; no bent or dog-eared corners; no store stamps on the covers or on inside pages; also called "pristine." |
| Excellent/B | The book may have been read once and might have small bends on the cover; no store stamps. |
| Very good/C | Might have a store stamp; has been read several times; yellowed pages; bent or dog-eared corners. |
| Good/D | Well-read; store stamp; yellowed pages; bent corners. |
| Fair-Poor/E | Dropped, kicked, beaten up. Read the book, then discard. |

All of the prices in our value section reflect A-B conditions. For excellent condition (B) books, deduct $1 for every $5 at which the book is valued. To calculate the price of a very good (C) condition books, deduct $2 for every $5. For good (D) condition books, deduct $3 for every $5. Fair/poor (E) condition books are not considered worth collecting *unless* the book is extremely rare. In that case, save the book until you can find another copy of it in better condition.

## CONSERVATION AND PRESERVATION GUIDELINES (OR HOW TO SAVE AND PROPERLY STORE YOUR BOOKS)

Because there are drastic changes in temperature, poor ventilation, humidity and possible water damage connected with basements and attics, we urge you never to store paperback novels (or hardcovers) in those areas of your home. Fire departments also advise that fires often begin in a basement or an attic where paper items (especially books) ignite faster due to poor ventilation. Most floods begin in basements. Even if you have never had an inch of standing water on your basement floor, you will feel dampness and moisture if you place your hand on your basement wall. These are two of paper's worst enemies.

Books should always be stored upright and, if possible, in plastic baggies (check with book searchers and dealers for these supplies), or in special book bags available from your local library. If your books are boxed, wrap plastic around the box. Make sure your bookcase shelves are level. If a shelf isn't level, it puts a great deal of strain on the books it holds; more often than not, your books will warp from being stored that way.

The perfect condition for storing books is in a well-ventilated room maintained at an even temperature (60-75 degrees) with approximately 50 percent humidity. Never place your bookcase in full sunlight. Also, check your volumes on a regular basis when you are dusting them—insects are attracted to the dye used on paperback covers and often can do lots of damage that isn't visible until you pull the books out.

### BOOK SAVING TIPS:

- If your novel has a store sticker on it, the best way to remove it is to use a blow dryer. Point the nozzle directly at the sticker and when it gets warm enough, it should be easier to peel off.

- If your books have bent covers, iron them under a piece of linen.

- To clean book covers, use a dust cloth or spray some Windex (lightly) on a towel. Never rub covers hard since they tend to peel.

- When you are reading a book, try not to bend the spine. Even though this is often difficult to avoid, a book with no creases or bends is more valuable than one which shows signs of having been well-read. Handle your book gently and it will last much longer. Remember, most romances weren't expected to become collector's items and, as a result, were published as paperbacks. Therefore, they require more care than books with leather bindings.

## KEEPING TRACK OF YOUR COLLECTION

It is important not only to preserve your books—you should also keep track of them. Since all books can be insured as collectibles, you should make a list, including title, author, edition, copyright date, publisher, edition and condition of the book. Appraisals of your collection can be performed by one of the Network book searchers at a cost of $20–$50 depending on the size and value of your collection. You can insure your collection simply by adding it to your homeowner's insurance policy. If you rent, you can obtain an apartment insurance policy. Photographing your collection using a still or video camera will ensure your collection is properly documented. Have a copy made of the photos, video, or computer disk. Keep one copy in a non-flammable box or file one in your home and store the other in your safe deposit box or with your attorney.

The Personal Book Collection is a home-based computer program that will catalog your books by author, title, or series name (e.g., Harlequin Presents or Silhouette Desire). The program is self-contained and the user should only have to input the individual book information, such as title, author, etc. It is possible to add or delete this information at any time. Reports print by author's name, title or series' name in numerical order. The program costs approximately $25 and is available through Twilight Publishing Group (their address is listed in Chapter 4).

## WHERE TO BUY ROMANCE NOVELS

Obviously, you must pick up the novel at a book-store in order to obtain a first edition. Recently some of the larger book selling chains have recently offered support to romance authors. For example, Waldenbooks arranges book signings for romance authors on a regular basis and calls itself "the romance bookstore." Not only do authors admire Waldenbooks for the special attention it gives them, but readers are beginning to realize that the chain is carrying romances and favorite romance authors as a regular specialty. Waldenbooks also publishes a monthly newsletter which reviews romances and is offered free to the chain's customers. (All addresses appear in Chapter 4.)

Other chains which have large romance sections include Barnes & Noble, Bookland (Books-a-Million), and B. Dalton. Bookland also publishes a newsletter and often reviews romances. As with Waldenbooks, the newsletter is free to Bookland's customers. (For addresses of these publications, please check Chapter 4.)

Groups of local romance writers often get together for "mall signings." This is the perfect way to meet three to five novelists at once. Bring plenty of cash to buy at least one book by each author who can then autograph your purchases. If you can, save the autographed copies for your collection and purchase used copies of the same books to read. You can always turn in your used copies to the used bookstore for more credit once you've read them.

Many of the larger publishers (e.g., Harlequin, Silhouette, Zebra, Avon, etc.) offer their customers service by mail order. Most of their books have a pull-out subscription card inside each volume which can be filled out and mailed to the publisher. Customers will either get an automatic shipment of new romances every month or will be offered the opportunity to order from a catalog. Some of the larger distributors (e.g., Ingram's) also offer their customers this option. Addresses for all of these companies are listed in Chapter 4 of this book.

Romance novelists truly appreciate the small bookstore owners who have been supportive of them. In fact, the Central Florida chapter of the Romance Writers of America (RWA) has given its members a list of "Bookstores That Care." *Romance Times* also has a list of such bookstores. Contact the magazine for further information. You'll find *Romantic Times* in the list provided in Chapter 4. The bookstores on that list are often sent pre-publication notices when the authors have new books coming out.

The small bookstore is more likely to cater to its customers' personal needs than a large chain. If the owner is familiar with an author's work, she or he will often notify regular customers when a new book by that author arrives. These bookstores are also able to order virtually any book in print for their customers and often do so at no charge. Making friends with your local bookstore owner is a great way to accumulate first editions. You might even be able to convince the bookstore owner to invite your favorite romance authors in for signings. The owner of a small bookstore is usually thrilled to have local or out-of-town authors visit for a day. It doesn't cost the owner anything except some time—unless they want to print some flyers to notify their favorite customers about the special occasion—and they often acquire new customers through such a promotion.

Used bookstores always have a large selection of romances on the shelves but since the owners know which books and authors will be purchased by their regular customers, it's wise to make your interests known to keep the owner apprised. She or he can then call you when one of your books arrives. Remember, when you buy from a used bookstore the book will be stamped, it will have been read previously and it will probably not be in the best condition. However, when you look for books by your favorite authors, used bookstores are often the only place to find them.

Mail order searchers are the people to contact if you're having problems finding particular titles or authors. These people do most of the work by phone or fax, thus their prices reflect the additional expense of searching out specific books. When they locate your book, it will be mailed via book rate, which takes six days to six weeks. If you make a special request, they will use a two-day priority mailing system. The books will be properly packaged in bubble wrap, padded envelopes or boxes stuffed with shredded newspapers or packing fill.

The hardest books to find seem to be the trilogies or sets. Thus, you need to be patient when filing such a request. Your list should be kept fairly small (ten or fewer books at a time). You should also include a self-addressed, stamped envelope and a note which includes your name, address and phone number. We suggest you write to one to three shops to get the broadest response and range of prices. Once the searcher locates the books, ask what condition the books are in. Keep track of how much you've paid for your books by keeping your receipts, as well as a list of what's in your collection (see the Conservation and Restoration section for further information).

If you live near a bookstore which provides a search service, the store will usually hold your books for fourteen to thirty days. If the books are not picked up by that time, they are returned to the vendor, whether it be another used bookstore or a distributor.

Readers' groups are another good way to find books. Most libraries or local bookstores can tell you about readers' groups in the area, and magazines like *Romantic Times* often do feature stories on groups throughout the country. The group usually trades books and often arranges to go to book signings or conventions together. Not only will you be exposed to a wide variety of books through a readers' group, you'll make some long-lasting friendships with people who share your interest in romance as well.

Finally, there are romance writer conventions throughout the country where readers are often welcome to participate in the large book signings held in conjunction with these meetings. *Romantic Times* sponsors a yearly convention where readers can rub elbows with literary stars for nearly a week. The 1994 convention was held in Nashville and the book signing event featured hundreds of popular authors—a reader's heaven. The Romance Writers of America also sponsors an annual event and regional conferences throughout the country. There are often autograph parties to which the public is invited. In addition, other romance writers' and readers' groups arrange annual get-togethers to which the public is invited. By staying in touch with your local bookstore, writers and readers' groups, and reading the magazines and newspapers published for the industry, you can keep abreast of such happenings and make sure you're part of them.

## How to Sell Romance Novels

When it comes time to sell part or all of your collection, remember that most used bookstores usually accept books on consignment, so you may not get paid immediately. If a dealer does buy your collection, you will usually get paid one-half of what the dealer can get for the book. Dealers have to consider their overhead and must make a profit on what they sell. Thus, all these considerations are factored into the purchase price.

Often a bookstore or a member of the search network will obtain a book and put it up for bid. The person who owns the book places an ad with the network indicating a base price, the bottom dollar the seller will accept for the book. Then the searcher (or whoever is conducting the bidding) will set a sixty-day period for bids to arrive. The people who bid usually forward their bids by mail or by fax; these are called sealed bids. When the sixty-day period has expired, the seller opens the bids and the book is awarded to the highest bidder. If two people have the same bid, the seller has the option of contacting the two highest bidders to see if either of them want to increase the bid.

Although most bidding is done in this manner, there are some exceptions. For instance, a store/searcher/seller may want to advise the top bidders of their respective bids so a bidder may offer a higher price. Recently, Kay Hooper's book *If There Be Dragons* was sold for more than its value because the buyers got into a bidding war.

When you get into a bidding situation, it behooves you to know the condition of the book and the people with whom you are dealing. This is yet another example of the old caveat "buyer beware." Also make sure you ask what arrangements will be made to forward the book to the highest bidder. Most reputable dealers/searchers/sellers will send the book via two-day priority mail once they have received payment.

Whenever you are dealing in collectibles, it is necessary to start with the premise that you must take care of yourself and your own needs. Just as an auctioneer will suggest that a "buyer beware", we ask you to take heed that not everyone who trades in the book business will be fair. Your best weapon against being cheated or defrauded is to educate yourself about the pitfalls of collecting. In many ways, this is the purpose of this book as well.

## CHAPTER 4

# THE ROMANCE COLLECTOR'S RESOURCE GUIDE

## ASSOCIATIONS AND ORGANIZATIONS INCLUDING READERS' GROUPS AND WRITERS' GROUPS

Although your local library or bookstore will usually have information available so you can contact the readers' and writers' groups in your area, there are larger groups which have recently formed that communicate via computer (i.e. GEnie, Prodigy). Of course, writers also have access to such groups as the Romance Writers of America; Novelists; Ink (part of GEnie); and the National Writers Union, among others.

The list below is a handy compilation of resources you might find useful in seeking out others who share your interest in romance collecting or in tracking down romance materials which are unavailable through libraries and bookstores in your area. If you're unable to find the information or books you want, check the magazines devoted to romance writing and reading for up-to-the-moment information.

## READERS' GROUPS/COMPUTER SERVICES

America On-Line (bulletin boards for both readers
and writers)
CompuServe (on-line romance readers group)
Genie (on-line readers group)
Prodigy (on-line bulletin board for readers/writers)

*Most of these on-line services have forums or
boards hosted by publishers where you can often
speak personally with authors or editors.

## WRITERS' GROUPS

The Authors Guild
330 W. 42nd Street
New York, NY 10036-6902

The Authors League of
America
330 W. 42nd Street
29th Floor
New York, NY 10036

Council of Authors &
Journalists
c/o Uncle Remus
Regional Library System
1131 East Avenue
Madison, GA 30650

International Women's
Writing Guild
Box 810, Gracie Station
New York, NY 10028

Mystery Writers of
America
17 E. 47th Street,
6th Floor
New York, NY 10017

National Writers Club
1450 S. Havana, Suite 620
Aurora, CO 80012

National Writers Union
873 Broadway, Rm. 203
New York, NY 10003

PEN American Center
568 Broadway
New York, NY 10012

Romance Writers of
America
13700 Veterans Memorial
Suite 315
Houston, TX 77014

Science Fiction Fantasy
Writers of America
5 Winding Brook Drive
Suite 1B
Guilderland, NY 12084

Women's National Book
Association
160 5th Avenue
New York, NY 10010

Writers Alliance
Box 2014
Setauket, NY  11733

Writer's Guild of
America (East)
555 W. 57th Street, #1230
New York, NY  10019

Writer's Guild of
America (West)
8955 Beverly Blvd.
Los Angeles, CA  90048

## REFERENCE BOOKS, MAGAZINES, NEWSLETTERS, CATALOGS, AND OTHER RESOURCES

* Author's note: All the reference materials listed in this section deal with books as collectibles, romance books in particular, reviews of romance books, or reading/writing romance novels. For further information, we suggest you write to the periodical or contact the publisher listed.

### BOOKS

*Essence of Romance*
(Twilight Publishing)

*Romance by the Numbers*, *Romance by the Title*, and *Romance by the Author*, all by Helen and Clair Gibson (Twilight Publishing)

*The Story Continues II*
Twilight Publishing Group
13519 Hooper Road
Baton Rouge, LA  70818

*Romantic Spirit* by Peggy J. Jaeghy (out of print but a searcher may be able to find a copy for you) (Rose Publishing)

*Romantic Hearts* by Peggy J. Jaeghy (Rose Publishing)

*Trudy's Time Periods*
(Bateman Publishing)

### BOOKSTORE PUBLICATIONS
#### (FREE AT BOOKSTORE CHAINS)

*Bookpage*
(BookLand/Books-a-Million stores)

*Heart to Heart*
(B. Dalton Bookstores)

*Romantic Reader*
(Waldenbooks)

## CATALOGS

*Alota Books*
P.O. Box 113
Joshua, TX  76058-0113

*Book Jackets*
P.O. Box 3077
Culver City, CA  90231

*Cy Publishing Group*
P.O. Box 1287
Lanham, MD  20703

*Gothic Journal*
19210 Forest Road, Rd. N.
Forest Lake, MN
55025

*Grace Livingston Hill
Readers Club*
c/o Tyndale House
Publications
351 Executive Drive
Carol Stream, IL 60188

*Hard to Find Books*
46229 287th Avenue S.E.
Enumclaw, WA  98022

*Manderley*
P.O. Box 880
Boonville, CA 95415-0880

*Old Book Barn Catalog*
Route 51 North
P.O. Box 500
Forsyth, IL  62535

*Puget Sound Readers
Newsletter*
2709 Bridgeport Way
W. #22
Tacoma, WA  98466

*The Radical Romantic*
Dept. RT,
12226 Pacific Avenue, #1
Mar Vista, CA 90066-4429

*Romantic Hearts
Newsletter*
P.O. Box 5951
Fort Hood, TX  76544

*Shamrock Enterprises
Romance Readers
Computer Bulletin Board*
P.O. Box 154
Champlin, MN  55316

*Time Travel & Occult
Romances*
P.O. Box 10146
Costa Mesa, CA  92627

*The Talisman*
P.O. Box 1641
Humble, TX 77347-1641

*Writer's Workshop Review*
1530 W. Clark Street, B
Pasco, WA  99301

## MAGAZINES

*Affair De Coeur*
1555 Washington Avenue
San Leandro, CA 94577

*American Collectors
Journal*
P.O. Box 407
Kewanee, IL 61443-0407

*Antique Trader Weekly*
P.O. Box 1050
Dubuque, IA 52004-1050

*Collector Editions*
Collector Communications
Corporation
170 5th Avenue
New York, NY 10010-5911

*Collectors News & The
Antique Reporter*
P.O. Box 156
Grundy Center, IA
50638-1056

*Gothic Journal*
9757 Janero Court, North
St. Paul, MN 55115-1339

*Paperback Reviews
Magazine*
P.O. Box 6781-RT
Albuquerque, NM 87197

*Publisher's Weekly*
P.O. Box 1979
Marion, OH 43302

*Romance Writer's Report*
Romance Writers of
America
13700 Veterans
Memorial Drive, Suite 315
Houston, TX 77014

*Romantic Times*
Romantic Times
Publishing Group
55 Bergen Street
Brooklyn Heights, NY
11201

*Yesteryear*
Yesteryear Publications
P.O. Box 2
Princeton, WI 54968

## NEWSLETTERS

*Facts for Fiction*
CMB Publications
4101 Green Oaks Blvd. W.
Suite 138
Arlington, TX 76016

*The Medieval Chronicle*
P.O. Box 1663
Carlsbad, CA 92018-1663

*Psychic Writer's Network*
119 Cregar Road
High Bridge, NJ 08829

*The Reader's Voice*
2646 Wyoming Avenue,
SW
Wyoming, MI 49509-2370

*The Regency Plume
Newsletter*
Box 870049
Mesquite, TX 75150

*Rendezvous*
1507 Burnham Avenue
Calumet City, IL 60409

*Romance Readers*
3402 Edgemont Avenue
Suite 331
Brookhaven, PA 19015-2804

*Rose Petals and Pearls*
P.O. Box 7082
Jackson, TN 38303

## TELEVISION SHOW (on collectibles)

FOX Network
Seth Katz
727 11th Avenue
New York, NY 10019

## CONFERENCES AND CONVENTIONS

*Each local Romance Writers of America chapter usually has a workshop or conference of their own. Contact the main office of the RWA to ask for the local chapter nearest you.

Affaire de Coeur
Magazine Annual
(Rom Con held annually
in California)

Romance Writers of
America
(1995 annual conference
scheduled for Hawaii)

*Romantic Times*
Convention—annual
convention for authors,
readers, booksellers,
agents, editors, etc.
(1994: scheduled for
Fort Worth, Texas;
1995: tentatively
scheduled for Europe)

## DIRECTORY OF GREAT AMERICAN BOOK SEARCH NETWORK

President:         Jacque Tiegs (708) 362-3021
                   (fax and phone)
Board members:  Helen Gibson, The Bookfinders
                   (504) 261-6832
                   Bev Estep, Second Chance Books
                   (206) 566-6545
Author liaison:   Maureen Wauksmith,
                    (206) 858-6880

Newsletter:      Maureen Wauksmith and
                 Jacque Tiegs (see above)
Membership:      Ann Hopgood, The Bookshop
                 (907) 248-4102

A Novel Idea
6310 Woodward
Downers Grove, IL  60516
Contact: Ron or Rita
Phone: (708) 963-8480

Alota Books
P.O. Box 113
Joshua, TX  76058-0113
Contact: Cristen
Phone: (817) 640-7006

Another Look Books
22153 Kings Court
Woodhaven, MI
48183-3213
Contact: Darlene Krogol
Phone (313) 676-5006

A to Z Books
1123 Grand
Grover Beach, CA  93433
Contact: Lara
Phone: (805) 489-8653

Bookfinders
14825 Central Woods
Avenue
Baton Rouge, LA  70818
Contact: Helen Gibson
Phone: (504) 261-6832

Booknook Repeats
7627 Sheridan Road
Kenosha, WI  53143
Contact: Nita
Phone: (414) 654-9221

Cheap Romance
7115 W. North Avenue
Suite 231
Oak Park, IL  60302
Contact: Susan Collins
Phone: (708) 383-6846
Voice Mail:
(708) 445-6256

Hard to Find Books
46229 287th Avenue, S.E.
Enumclaw, WA  98022
Contact: Sandy Heeter
Phone: (206) 825-6802

Highland Book Rack, Inc.
509 N. Main Street
Highlands, TX
77562-2221
Contact: Kenneth
& Lena McCann
Network Computer
Director
Phone/Fax:
(713) 843-2434

Mad About Books
1425 Golf Road
Waukegan, IL  60087
Contact: Brenda
Phone: (708) 244-8495

Old Book Barn
Route 51
Forsyth, IL  62535
Contact: Cheryl
Phone: (217) 875-0222

Pages Etc.
423 Court, #2
Saginaw, MI 48602
Contact: Jackie Skimson
Phone: (517) 792-3804

Paperback Cottage
129 Main Street
P.O. Box 283
South Dennis, MA
02660
Contact: Joan Sullivan
Phone: (508) 760-2101
Fax: (508) 760-2103

Patti's Books
P.O. Box 26566
Akron, OH 44319
Contact: Patti
Phone/Fax: (216) 644-2112

Previously Owned Books
103 S.W. Fremont #195
Selah, WA 98942
Contact: Vicky
Phone: (509) 697-4822
or (509) 577-0517
Fax: (509) 697-8885

Readers Haven, Inc.
815 South Charles
Elgin, IL 60120
Contact: Lynda J. Young
Phone: (708) 697-2526
Fax: (708) 924-7804

Sandpiper Books
746 Drury Court
Gurnee, IL 60033
Contact: Jacque Tiegs
Phone/Fax:
(708) 362-3021

Second Chance Books
2709 Bridgeport Way W.,
#22
Tacoma, WA 98466
Contact: Bev or Maureen
Phone: (206) 566-5545
Fax: (206) 858-6830

The Book Bug
354 Kingsway Mall
Siketon, MI 63801
Contact: Joyce
Phone: (314) 471-2042

The Book Exchange
13337 Midlothian
Turnpike
Midlothian, VA 23113
Contact: Martha
Phone: (804) 748-5702
Fax: (804) 378-6072

The Bookshop
750 W. Dimond,
#102-103
Anchorage, AL 99515
Contact: Ann Hopgood
Phone/Fax:
(907) 248-1940
Phone/Fax:
(907) 344-1940

Turn the Page, Inc.
39469 Joy Road
Canton, MI 48187
Contact: Joanne
or Dawn
Phone: (313) 459-7680

# QUICK REFERENCE

## CHAPTER 5

## ROMANCE NOVEL PRICES— WHAT IS YOUR BOOK WORTH?

Before diving headlong into what you've been waiting for—the value of the books you've been collecting—we'd like to offer a few words of explanation and guidance about the value of your romance collectibles.

First, the values listed below are for books in excellent to mint condition. If the book is in good condition, the price will decrease by 25 percent; if in fair condition, the book will be worth 50 percent of its price in the following list. A book in poor condition has almost no value for collecting purposes, unless it is a rare book; then it would be worth approximately one-third of the value listed.

Second, certain books and authors are more in demand in different areas of the country, as we discussed in Market Trends in Chapter 3. You may be able to more easily find works by certain authors in your part of the country. This will affect the value of their books, making them less valuable where those authors' books are difficult to find. When you are unable to find your favorite authors, the value of their books will increase.

Third, this list is intended simply as a guide. It is not written in stone, gold, or blood. The prices are only meant to give you an idea of what the books might be worth. These prices are variable and could change tomorrow; the author's works may suddenly become more valuable or the line may decrease in popularity for reasons no one can anticipate today.

With this in mind, remember that a book—or any collectible, for that matter—is only worth what the last person paid for it. So, have fun and good luck finding a treasure!

## Values of Imprints

In the publishing industry, a series of books, e.g., Harlequin Intrigue or Candlelight Ecstasy, is called an imprint. Among romance readers and collectors, these series are also known as "lines." We use these terms interchangeably in discussing book values.

Some imprints have been discontinued, yet their popularity continues. Other imprints are extremely collectible because they were printed in small quantities. The examples listed below are a few of the imprints which book searchers are currently being asked to find. If you discover the imprint you are collecting is not listed, please contact a book searcher in the Network so we can update our information.

**American Indian Series (1-14)**
 (various authors)            $ 5.00 each
**Birthstone Gothic Series (1-12)**
 (various authors)            75.00 set
**Cameo Gothic Series**
 (various authors)            5.00 each
**Delaney and Shamrock Series
(14 books)**            100.00 set
 (authors: Johansen, Preston, Hooper)
**Duets (1-6)**            10.00 each
**Falconhurst Series (1-14)**
 (various authors)            75.00 each
**Leather and Lace Series**            5.00 each
 (authors: Dixon, Armstrong, Lee)

| | | |
|---|---|---|
| **Collection '86 Silhouette Christmas Stories** | $ 5.00 each | |
| **Collection '87 Silhouette Christmas Stories** | 10.00 each | |
| **Women of the West Series** (various authors) | 5.00 each | |
| **Zodiac Gothic Series** | 5.00 each | |

## *Value List by Author*

Obviously, the list below is not all-inclusive. For example, some very popular authors are not listed at all because their books are still available in mass quantities and, therefore, have not yet become collectible. The books and authors listed here are the ones we have found collectors and readers have been searching for through bookstores listed on the Network. As more collectors connect through book searchers, computer networking, word of mouth, conferences and reading groups, we are confident this list will rapidly expand.

If you have a question about a certain author or book, please contact one of the bookstores listed in the directory, contact *Romantic Times* for their list of "Bookstores That Care," or write to us through Alliance Publishing.

The prices we have listed here are for paperback versions of books unless otherwise specified. If the book has been reissued, we have either noted that there is a new version or we have not included that reissue on the list.

### KEY:

| | |
|---|---|
| CAN | Candlelight |
| CE | Candlelight Ecstasy |
| COLL | Collection |
| CONT | Contemporary (general-big books) |
| CR | Candlelight Regencies |
| CS | Candlelight Ecstasy Supreme |
| DELAN | Delaney & Shamrock |
| DELL/B | Dell's Maggie Bennett Series |

| | |
|---|---|
| F | Futuristic (includes fantasy) |
| GLN | Gallen |
| GOTH | Gothic |
| HAR | Harlequin |
| HC | Hardcover |
| HH | Harlequin Historical |
| HI | Harlequin Intrigue |
| HIST | Historical (general-big books) |
| HM | Harlequin Masquerade |
| HP | Harlequin Presents |
| JONES | Jones |
| JUV | Juvenile |
| K | Kismet/Meteor |
| LS | Loveswept |
| LSS | Loveswept Specials |
| M & B | Mills & Boon |
| MF | MacFadden |
| MYST | Mysteries |
| R | Regencies |
| SC | Second Chance at Love |
| SD | Silhouette Desire |
| SE | Silhouette Special Edition |
| SIM | Silhouette Intimate Moments |
| SINSP | Silhouette Inspirationals |
| SR | Silhouette Romance |
| SS | Silhouette Shadows |
| SSE | Silhouette Special Editions |
| T | Topaz |
| TT | Time Travel |
| WF | Wildfire (teen romances) |
| WOM/WEST | Women of the West |

| AUTHOR LINE/# | TITLE | VALUE |
|---|---|---|
| Anderson, Catherine | | |
| HIST | *Comanche Moon* | $4.00 |
| HIST | *Comanche Heart* | $4.00 |
| HIST | *Indigo Blue* | $4.00 |
| Archer, Jane | | |
| HIST | *Rebellious Rapture* | $4.00 |
| HIST | *Silken Spurs* | $5.00 |

|       |                          |            |
|-------|--------------------------|------------|
| HIST  | *Satin & Silver*         | $4.00      |
| HIST  | *Spring Dreams*          | $4.00      |

**Baker, Madeline**
| TT | *Love in the Wind* | $4.00 |

**Bale, Karen A.**
| HIST | *Sweet Medicine* | |
| Prophecy Series/each | | $5.00 |

**Balogh, Mary**
| R | *Masked Deception, A*   | $4.00 |
| R | *Web of Love*           | $3.00 |
| R | *Chance Encounter, A*   | $3.00 |
| R | *Wood Nymph, The*       | $3.00 |
| R | *Devil Web, The*        | $3.00 |
| R | *Trysting Place, The*   | $3.00 |

**Barclay, Suzanne**
| HH 141 | *Knight Dreams*  | $3.00 |
| HH 162 | *Knight's Lady*  | $3.00 |
| HH 184 | *Knight's Honor* | $3.00 |

**Barkin, Jill**
| CONT | *Hot Streak* | $20.00 |

**Barnett, Jill**
| HIST | *Just a Kiss Away* | $6.00 |
| HIST | *Bewitching*       | $6.00 |
| HIST | *Heart's Haven*    | $6.00 |

**Bentley, Jayne**
| MF 192 | *Moment Past Midnight*  | $150–250 |
| MF 224 | *Turning Towards Home*  | $150–200 |
| MF 249 | *Maiden of the Morning* | $150–250 |
|        | (3-book reprint/each)   | $100.00  |

**Bittner, Roseanne**
| HIST | *Savage Destiny* (set) | $18.00 |

**Blayne, Diana**
| CE 94   | *Waiting Game, A*        | $10.00 |
| CE 113  | *Loving Arrangement, A*  | $10.00 |
| CE 138  | *White Sand, Wild Sea*   | $5.00  |
| CE 184  | *Dark Surrender*         | $5.00  |
| CES 49  | *Color Love Blue*        | $20.00 |
| CES 110 | *Tangled Destinies*      | $5.00  |

F. Rosanne Bittner's *Savage Destiny* set,
including *Sweet Prairie Passion*, *Ride the
Free Wind (#2)* and *Meet the New Dawn (#6)*.
Courtesy of Jacque Tiegs.

## Boswell, Barbra

| LS 53 | *Little Consequences* | $8.00 |
| LS 78 | *Sensuous Perception* | $8.00 |

## Brown, Sandra

| HAR 1 | *Tomorrow's Promise* | $3.00 |
| LS 1 | *Heaven's Price* | $10.00 |
| LS 22 | *Breakfast in Bed* | $5.00 |
| LS 51 | *Send No Flowers* | $4.00 |
| LS 66 | *In a Class by Itself* | $2.50 |
| LS 79 | *Thursday's Child* | $10.00 |
| LS 115 | *Riley in the Morning* | $5.00 |
| LS 136 | *Rana Look, The* | $5.00 |
| LS 154 | *22 Indigo Place* | $5.00 |
| LS 185 | *Sunny Chandler's Return* | $5.00 |
| LS 197 | *Demon Rumm* | $5.00 |
| LS 217 | *Fanta C* | $4.00 |
| LS 229 | *Tidings of Great Joy* | $3.00 |
| LS 263 | *Hawk O'Toole's Hostage* | $4.00 |
| LS 300 | *Long Time Coming* | $2.50 |
| LS 336 | *Temperatures Rising* | $2.50 |
| LS 366 | *Whole New Light, A* | $2.50 |
| SD 106 | *Relentless Desire* | $6.00 |
| SD 137 | *Temptation's Kiss* | $6.00 |

## Cartland, Barbara

| R HC | *Chieftain Without a Heart, The* | $10.00 |

| | | |
|---|---|---|
| R | *Fire of Love, The* (English) | $3.00 |
| R | *Complacent Wife, The* | $3.00 |
| R | *Pretty Horsebreakers, The* | $3.00 |

**Castle, Jayne**

| | | |
|---|---|---|
| CE 2 | *Gentle Pirate* | $10.00 |
| CE 17 | *Wagered Weekend* | $10.00 |
| CE 23 | *Right of Possession* | $10.00 |
| CE 26 | *Bargain with the Devil* | $10.00 |
| CE 36 | *Man's Protection, A* | $10.00 |
| CE 45 | *Relentless Adversary* | $10.00 |
| CE 55 | *Affair of Risk* | $10.00 |
| CE 68 | *Negotiated Surrender, A* | $10.00 |
| CE 79 | *Power Play* | $10.00 |
| CE 91 | *Spellbound* | $10.00 |
| CE 130 | *Conflict of Interest* | $10.00 |
| CONT | *Double Dealing* | $10.00 |
| JONES | *Chilling Deception, The* | $25.00 |
| JONES | *Desperate Game, The* | $25.00 |
| JONES | *Fatal Fortune, The* | $25.00 |
| JONES | *Sinister Touch, The* | $25.00 |
| MF 132 | *Vintage of Surrender* | $100.00 |
| MF 157 | *Queen of Hearts* | $100.00 |
| MF | (3-book reprint/each) | $100.00 |

**Chase, Elaine Raco**

| | | |
|---|---|---|
| CAN | *Special Delivery* | $3.00 |

**Chesney, Marion**

| | | |
|---|---|---|
| R | *Education of Miss Patterson, The* | $4.00 |
| R | *Taming of Annabelle, The* | $4.00 |

**Coffman, Virginia**

| | |
|---|---|
| any Gothic | $4.00–5.00 |

**Coulter, Catherine**

| | | |
|---|---|---|
| SSE 331 | *Aristocrat, The* | $5.00 |

**Curtis, Sharon/Tom**

| | | |
|---|---|---|
| LS 25 | *Lightning That Lingers* | $3.00 |

**Dailey, Janet**

| | | |
|---|---|---|
| HP | *Show Me* | $3.00 |
| HP | *Land Called Deseret, A* | $3.00 |
| HP | *That Boston Man* | $3.00 |

Dancer, Lacey
| | | |
|---|---|---|
| K 7 | *Silent Enchantment* | $6.00 |
| K 35 | *Diamond on Ice* | $6.00 |
| K 49 | *Sunlight on Shadows* | $6.00 |
| K 59 | *13 Days of Luck* | $6.00 |
| K 77 | *Flight of the Swan* | $6.00 |
| K 98 | *Baby Makes Five* | $6.00 |
| K 127 | *Forever Joy* | $6.00 |
| K 133 | *Lightning Strikes Twice* | $6.00 |
| K 163 | *His Womens' Gift* | $10.00 |
| K | *Pink Gift Set* (5)/each | $6.00 |

Deveraux, Jude
| | | |
|---|---|---|
| HIST | *Casa Grande* | $20.00 |

Drake, Bonnie
| | | |
|---|---|---|
| CE | All titles | $2.00 |

Drake, Shannon
| | | |
|---|---|---|
| HIST | *Ondine* | $5.00 |
| HIST | *Blue Heaven, Black Night* | $5.00 |
| HIST | *Emerald Embrace* | $5.00 |
| HIST | *Princess of Fire* | $5.00 |
| HIST | *Lie Down in Roses* | $5.00 |
| HIST | *Bride of the Wind* | $5.00 |

*Group by Lacey Dancer (notice difference in Kismet covers—
all in the group were published by Kismet):* Flight of the
Swan, Silent Enchantment, 13 Days of Luck, Diamond
on Ice, Lightning Strikes Twice *(#133),* Sunlight on
Shadows, *and a second version of* Diamond on Ice *in black
cover, #35. Courtesy of Jacque Tiegs.*

*Group by Jude Deveraux, including:* Casa Grande *(Avon),*
The Black Lyon *(Avon), and* Twin of Fire *(Avon).*
*Courtesy of Jacque Tiegs*

Eagle, Kathleen
    HH 2    *Private Treaty*    $4.00
    HH 30    *Medicine Man*    $5.00
    HH 50    *Heaven and Earth*    $4.00

Edwards, Cassie
    T    *Desires Blossom*    $4.00
    T    *Elusive Ecstasy*    $4.00
    T    *Enchanted Enemy*    $4.00
    T    *Eugenie's Embrace*    $4.00
    T    *Forbidden Embrace*    $4.00
    T    *Love's Legacy*    $4.00
    T    *Passion's Web*    $4.00
    T    *Portrait of Desire*    $5.00
    T    *Rapture's Rendevous*    $4.00
    T    *Savage Eden*    $4.00
    T    *Savage Obsession*    $4.00
    T    *Savage Splendor*    $4.00
    T    *Savage Torment*    $4.00
    T    *Secrets of My Heart*    $4.00

Faith, Barbara
    GLN    *Kill Me Gently, Darling*    $20.00
    GLN    *Moonkissed, The*    $5.00
    GLN    *Sundancer's, The*    $5.00

Faye, Dyer Lois
    K 4    *Winterfire*    $4.00

| K 21 | *That James Boy* | $4.00 |
| K 70 | *Sunday Kind of Love* | $4.00 |
| K 88 | *More Than a Memory* | $4.00 |
| K 106 | *Traveling Man* | $4.00 |

**Feather, Jane**
| HIST | *Beloved Enemy* | $4.00 |
| HIST | *Bold Destiny* | $4.00 |
| HIST | *Brazen Whispers* | $4.00 |

**Garlock, Dorothy**
| LS 6 | *Love for All Time, A* | $3.00 |
| LS 33 | *The Planting Season* | $3.00 |
| GLN | *The Searching Hearts* | $10.00 |

**Garwood, Julie**
| WF | *Girl Named Summer* | $25.00 |
| | * teen romance | |

**Gentry, Georgina**
| COLL | *1991 Christmas Rendevous* | $5.00 |
| HIST | *Bandit's Embrace* | $4.00 |
| HIST | *Cheyenne Captive* | $4.00 |
| HIST | *Cheyenne Caress* | $6.00 |
| HIST | *Cheyenne Princess* | $7.00 |
| HIST | *Comanche Cowboy* | $10.00 |
| HIST | *Sioux Slave* | $4.00 |

**Glass, Amanda**
| F | *Shield's Lady* | $25.00 |

**Graham, Heather**
| HIST | *Devil's Mistress* | $5.00 |
| CE 94 | *An Angel Share* | $5.00 |
| CE 117 | *When Next We Meet* | $3.00 |
| CE 125 | *Tender Taming* | $4.00 |
| CE 154 | *Season of Love, A* | $4.00 |
| CE 214 | *Tender Deception* | $4.00 |
| CE 241 | *Hours to Cherish* | $4.00 |
| CE 271 | *Serena's Magic* | $4.00 |
| CE 359 | *Sensuous Angel* | $5.00 |
| CS 1 | *Tempestuous Eden* | $4.00 |
| CS 10 | *Night Sea and Stars* | $4.00 |
| CS 17 | *Red Midnight* | $4.00 |
| CS 37 | *Arabian Nights* | $4.00 |

| CS 67 | *Queen of Hearts* | $4.00 |
| CS 108 | *Dante's Daughter* | $4.00 |
| CS 127 | *Handful of Dreams* | $4.00 |

Gray, Ginna
| SSE 416 | *Fools Rush In* | $8.00 |
| SSE 468 | *Where Angels Fear* | $8.00 |

Hatcher, Robin Lee
| WOM/WEST | *Devlin's Promise* | $4.00 |
| WOM/WEST | *Promise Me Spring* | $4.00 |
| WOM/WEST | *Promise Sunrise* | $4.00 |

Henley, Virginia
| HIST | *Bold Conquest* | $5.00 |
| HIST | *Irish Gypsy* | $10.00 |
| HIST | *Wild Heart*s | $5.00 |

Heyer, Georgette
| R | *The Masqueraders* | $3.00 |
| | (all other Heyer titles) | $3.00 |

Hoag, Tami
| HIST | *Stillwater* | $4.00 |
| LS | *Sarah's Sin* | $4.00 |

Hohl, Joan
| SC 450 | *Window on Yesterday* | $4.00 |
| SC 454 | *Window on Today* | $4.00 |

*Virginia Henley's*
Bold Conquest *(Avon).*
Courtesy of Jacque Tiegs.

*Tami Hoag's* Sarah's Sin
*(Loveswept, #480).*
Courtesy of Jacque Tiegs.

| SD 458 | *Window on Tomorrow* | $4.00 |
| SSE 54 | *Thorn's Way* | $3.00 |
| SSE 537 | *Thorn's Wife* | $3.00 |

**Hooper, Kay**

| F | *Summer of the Unicorn* | $5.00 |
| CR 665 | *Lady Thief* | $40.00 |
| CE 153 | *On Wings of Magic* | $10–20 |
| LS 62 | *Pepper's Way* | $10.00 |
| LS 71 | *If There Be Dragons* | $20.00 |
| LS 83 | *Ill Possession* | $8.00 |
| LS 189 | *In Serena's Web* | $20.00 |
| LS 193 | *Raven on the Wing* | $10.00 |
| LS 221 | *Rafferty's Wife* | $4.00 |
| LS 225 | *Zach's Law* | $10.00 |
| LS 231 | *Fall of Lucas Kendrick, The* | $6.00 |
| LS 237 | *Unmasking Kelsey* | $5.00 |
| LS 286 | *Shades of Gray* | $4.00 |
| LS 296 | *Captain's Paradise* | $4.00 |
| LS 312 | *It Takes a Thief* | $4.00 |
| LS 321 | *Aces High* | $4.00 |
| DELAN | *Golden Flames* | $4.00 |
| DELAN | *Velvet Lightning* | $4.00 |
| DELAN | *Enchantress Adelaide, The* | $6.00 |
| SIM 297 | *Enemy Mine* | $4.00 |
| SIM 388 | *Haviland Touch, The* | $4.00 |

**Howard, Linda**

| SE 452 | *White Lies* | $6.00 |
| SIM 22 | *Against the Rules* | $8.00 |
| SIM 92 | *Tears of the Renegade* | $10.00 |
| SIM 129 | *Midnight Rainbow* | $20.00 |
| SIM 177 | *Diamond Bay* | $6.00 |
| SIM 201 | *Heartbreaker* | $10.00 |
| SIM 281 | *Mackenzie's Mountain* | $3.00 |
| SIM 349 | *Duncan's Bride* | $5.00 |
| SSE 22 | *All That Glitters* | $6.00 |
| SSE 46 | *An Independent Wife* | $5.00 |
| SSE 177 | *Come Lie with Me* | $10.00 |
| SSE 230 | *Sarah's Child* | $15.00 |
| SSE 260 | *Cutting Edge, The* | $5.00 |
| SSE 445 | *Mackenzie's Mission* | $3.00 |

**James, Kristin**

| GLN | *Summer Sky* | $5.00 |
| GLN | *Sapphire Sky* | $5.00 |

*Linda Howard's* Mackenzie's Mountain
*(Silhouette Intimate Moments #281), and*
Mackenzie's Mission *(Silhouette Intimate
Moments, #445).* Courtesy of Jacque Tiegs.

*Three novels by Linda Howard, including: a Christmas
promotional gift from Harlequin,* Bluebird in Winter;
Midnight Rainbow *(Silhouette Intimate Moments, #129);
and* Sarah's Child *(Silhouette Special Edition, #230).*
Courtesy of Jacque Tiegs.

|  |  |  |
|---|---|---|
| GLN | *Golden Sky* | $5.00 |
| SIM 17 | *Amber Sky* | $5.00 |

James, Stephanie

|  |  |  |
|---|---|---|
| SD XX | *Saxon's Lady* | $50.00 |
| SD 1 | *Corporate Affair* | $3.00 |
| SD 11 | *Velvet Touch* | $3.00 |
| SD 19 | *Lover in Pursuit* | $3.00 |
| SD 25 | *Renaissance Man* | $3.00 |
| SD 31 | *Reckless Passion* | $3.00 |
| SD 37 | *Price of Surrender* | $3.00 |
| SD 49 | *Affair of Honor* | $3.00 |

| | | |
|---|---|---|
| SD 55 | *To Tame the Hunter* | $3.00 |
| SD 67 | *Gamemaster* | $3.00 |
| SD 85 | *Silver Snare, The* | $3.00 |
| SD 97 | *Battle Prize* | $3.00 |
| SD 103 | *Body Guard* | $3.00 |
| SD 115 | *Gambler's Woman* | $3.00 |
| SD 127 | *Fabulous Beast* | $3.00 |
| SD 145 | *Night of the Magician* | $3.00 |
| SD 163 | *Nightwalker* | $3.00 |
| SD 187 | *Devil to Pay, The* | $3.00 |
| SD 211 | *Wizard* | $6.00 |
| SD 235 | *Golden Goddess* | $3.00 |
| SD 253 | *Cautious Lover* | $3.00 |
| SD 277 | *Green Fire* | $3.00 |
| SD 307 | *Second Wife* | $3.00 |
| SD 342 | *Challonder Bride, The* | $3.00 |
| SIM 9 | *Serpent in Paradise* | $6.00 |
| SIM 21 | *Raven Prey* | $6.00 |
| SIM 89 | *Passionate Business* | $5.00 |
| SSE 15 | *Dangerous Magic* | $6.00 |
| SSE 35 | *Stormy Challenge* | $6.00 |

Johansen, Iris

| | | |
|---|---|---|
| LS XX | *One Touch of Topaz* | $5.00 |
| LS 14 | *Stormy Vows* | $10.00 |
| LS 17 | *Tempest at Sea* | $6.00 |
| LS 24 | *Reluctant Lark* | $6.00 |
| LS 27 | *Bronzed Hawk* | $6.00 |
| LS 29 | *Lady and the Unicorn, The* | $8.00 |
| LS 31 | *Golden Valkyrie, The* | $20.00 |
| LS 35 | *Trustworthy Redhead, The* | $10.00 |
| LS 40 | *Return to Santa Flores* | $10.00 |
| LS 44 | *No Red Roses* | $10.00 |
| LS 55 | *Capture the Rainbow* | $4.00 |
| LS 59 | *Touch the Horizon* | $4.00 |
| LS 82 | *White Satin* | $4.00 |
| LS 86 | *Blue Velvet* | $4.00 |
| LS 122 | *Summer Smile, A* | $4.00 |
| LS 126 | *And the Desert Blooms* | $4.00 |
| LS 148 | *Always* | $4.00 |
| LS 152 | *Everlasting* | $4.00 |
| LS 168 | *Renegade York, The* | $5.00 |
| LS 176 | *Til the End of Time* | $4.00 |

*Iris Johansen's* No Red Roses *(Loveswept, #44) and* One Touch of Topaz *(Loveswept Special Edition—not for sale—by subscription only). Courtesy of Jacque Tiegs.*

*Iris Johansen's* Capture the Rainbow *(two different versions—originally published as #55).* Courtesy of Jacque Tiegs.

| LS 187 | *Last Bridge Home, The* | $4.00 |
| LS 191 | *Across the River of Yesterday* | $4.00 |
| LS 221 | *Spellbinder* | $4.00 |
| LS 232 | *Star Light, Star Bright* | $4.00 |
| LS 257 | *Man From Half-Moon Bay* | $4.00 |
| LS 342 | *Magnificent Folly* | $4.00 |
| LS 364 | *Wicked Jake Darcy* | $4.00 |
| LS 420 | *Tender Savage* | $3.00 |
| DELAN | *Satin Ice* | $5.00 |
| DELAN | *Wild Silver* | $4.00 |
| DELAN | *Adventuress Matilda, The* | $4.00 |
| DELAN | *This Fierce Splendor* | $6.00 |

Johnson, Susan

| | | |
|---|---|---|
| HH 51 | *Golden Paradise* | $10.00 |
| JUV | *Play, The* | $100.00 |
| HIST | *Honey Bear, The* (originally *Hot Streak*) | $10.00 |
| HIST | *Forbidden* | $5.00 |
| HIST | *Seized by Love* | $10.00 |
| HIST | *Love Storm* | $10.00 |

Johnston, Joan

| | | |
|---|---|---|
| HIST | *Comanche Woman* | $5.00 |
| HIST | *Coulter Wife* | $10.00 |
| HIST | *Frontier Woman* | $5.00 |
| HIST | *Texas Woman* | $5.00 |

Jordan, Laura

| | | |
|---|---|---|
| GLN | *Silken Web, The* | $6.00 |
| GLN | *Hidden Fires* | $10.00 |

Joyce, Brenda

| | | |
|---|---|---|
| CONT | *Lovers and Liars* | $10.00 |
| HIST | *Firestorm* | $15.00 |
| HIST | *Innocent Fire* | $20.00 |
| HIST | *Dark Fires* | $5.00 |
| HIST | *Scandalous Love* | $5.00 |
| HIST | *Darkest Heart* | $5.00 |
| HIST | *Fires of Paradise, The* | $5.00 |
| HIST | *Violet Fire* | $15.00 |
| HIST | *Conqueror, The* | $5.00 |

Kimbrough, Kathryn

| | | |
|---|---|---|
| GOTH | *Phenwick Woman Saga* (40-book set) | $100.00 |

Krentz, Jayne Ann

| | | |
|---|---|---|
| HI 10 | *Legacy, The* | $25.00 |
| HT 11 | *Uneasy Alliance* | $4.00 |
| HT 17 | *Waiting Game, The* | $25.00 |
| HI 21 | *Call it Destiny* | $4.00 |
| HT 34 | *Ghost of a Chance* | $6.00 |
| HT 74 | *Witchcraft* | $4.00 |
| HT 91 | *True Colors* | $4.00 |
| HT 109 | *Ties That Bind, The* | $4.00 |
| HT 125 | *Between the Lines* | $4.00 |

| HT 146 | *Family Way, The* | $4.00 |
| HT 157 | *Main Attraction, The* | $4.00 |
| HT 168 | *Chance of a Lifetime* | $4.00 |
| HT 177 | *Test of Time* | $4.00 |
| HT 191 | *Full Bloom* | $4.00 |
| HT 219 | *Joy* | $4.00 |
| HT 229 | *Dreams, Part One* | $6.00 |
| HT 230 | *Dreams, Part Two* | $6.00 |
| HT 241 | *Woman's Touch, A* | $4.00 |
| HT 270 | *Lady's Choice* | $4.00 |
| HT 287 | *Pirate, The* | $8.00 |
| HT 293 | *Adventurer, The* | $8.00 |
| HT 302 | *Cowboy, The* | $8.00 |
| HT 341 | *Too Wild to Wed?* | $4.00 |
| HT 365 | *Wedding Night, The* | $4.00 |
| HT 377 | *Private Eye, The* | $4.00 |
| CONT | *Sweet Starfire* | $10.00 |
| CONT | *Gift of Gold* | $6.00 |
| CONT | *Midnight Jewels* | $10.00 |
| CONT | *Twist of Fate* | $10.00 |
| CONT | *Gift of Fire* | $6.00 |
| CONT | *Coral Kiss* | $8.00 |

Kyle, Susan

| CONT | *Diamond Spur* | $10.00 |
| CONT | *Escapade* | $5.00 |
| CONT | *Firebrand* | $5.00 |
| SCI/FI | *Morci Battalion* | $500.00 |
| CONT | *Night Fever* | $5.00 |
| CONT | *True Colors* | $5.00 |

Lamb, Arnette

| HIST | *Threads of Destiny* | $5.00 |

Lee, Rachel

| SS | *Imminent Thunder* | $5.00 |
| SIM 449 | *Exile's End* | $6.00 |
| SIM 463 | *Cherokee Thunder* | $6.00 |
| SIM 482 | *Miss Emmaline and the Dark Angel* | $6.00 |
| SIM 494 | *Ironheart* | $2.99 |
| SIM 535 | *Lost Warriors* | $2.99 |

*Rachel Lee's* Cherokee Thunder *(Silhouette Intimate Moments American Hero series, #463).* From the collection of Peg Reno.

London, Laura

| CR 227 | *Heart Too Proud, A* | $5.00 |
| CR 255 | *Bad Barron's Daughter* | $5.00 |
| CR 263 | *Moonlight Mist* | $5.00 |
| CR 565 | *Love's a Stage* | $5.00 |
| CR 644 | *Gypsy Heiress, The* | $5.00 |
| HIST | *Windflower* | $7.00 |

Lorin, Amii

| CE 1 | *Tawny Gold Man, The* | $5.00 |
| CE 7 | *Game is Played, The* | $4.00 |
| CE 11 | *Morgan Wade's Woman* | $4.00 |
| CE 22 | *Breeze Off the Ocean* | $4.00 |
| CE 50 | *Snowbound Weekend* | $4.00 |
| CE 99 | *Gambler's Love* | $4.00 |

*Amii Lorin's* Night Striker *(Candlelight Ecstasy Supreme, #113) and* Powder and Seduction *(Candlelight Ecstasy, #391).* Courtesy of Jacque Tiegs.

| CE 391 | Power and Seduction | $4.00 |
| CES 32 | While the Fire Rages | $4.00 |
| CES 113 | Night Striker | $4.00 |
| M&B/HC | Candleglow | $50.00 |

Lowell, Elizabeth

| CONT | Tell Me No Lies | $3.00 |
| SD 77 | Summer Thunder | $5.00 |
| SD 265 | Fires of Spring, The | $5.00 |
| SD 319 | Too Hot to Handle | $5.00 |
| SD 355 | Love Song for a Raven | $5.00 |
| SD 415 | Fever | $5.00 |
| SD 462 | Dark Fire | $5.00 |
| SD 546 | Fire and Rain | $5.00 |
| SD 624 | Outlaw | $5.00 |
| SD 625 | Granite Man | $5.00 |
| SD 631 | Warrior | $5.00 |
| SIM 18 | Danver's Touch | $5.00 |
| SIM 34 | Lover in the Rough | $8.00 |
| SIM 57 | Summer Games | $5.00 |
| SIM 72 | Forget Me Not | $5.00 |
| SIM 81 | Woman Without Lies, A | $8.00 |
| SIM 97 | Traveling Man | $5.00 |
| SIM 109 | Valley of the Sun | $8.00 |
| SIM 128 | Sequel | $5.00 |
| SIM 141 | Fires of Eden | $5.00 |
| SIM 178 | Sweet Wind, Wild Wind | $4.00 |
| SIM 256 | Chain Lightning | $5.00 |

Macomber, Debbie

| SINSP 1 | Heartsong | $10.00 |
| SINSP 9 | Undercover Dreamer | $10.00 |
| SINSP 15 | A Girl Like Janet | $10.00 |
| SINSP 21 | Thanksgiving Prayer | $20.00 |
| SINSP 23 | Gift of Christmas, The | $20.00 |
| SINSP 29 | Love Thy Neighbor | $10.00 |
| SSE 494 | Navy Wife | $4.00 |
| SSE 518 | Navy Blues | $4.00 |
| SSE 662 | Navy Brat | $4.00 |
| SSE 683 | Navy Woman | $4.00 |
| SSE 697 | Navy Baby | $4.00 |

Mason, Connie

| WOM/WEST | Beyond the Horizon | 4.00 |

Maxwell, Ann
  SCI/FI    *Singer Enigma*              $50.00
  SCI/FI    *Dancer Series (per book)*   $25.00
  SCI/FI    *Name of a Shadow*           $30.00
  SCI/FI    *Change*                     $50.00

Maxwell, A. E.
  MYST      *Fiddler and Flora Series*   $5.00/ea.
  MYST      *Empire Series*              $8.00

McBain, Laurie
  HIST      *Dark Before the Rising Sun*   $4.00

O'Banyon, Constance
            Savage Season Set:
  HIST      *Savage Spring*     $5.00
  HIST      *Savage Summer*     $5.00
  HIST      *Savage Autumn*     $5.00
  HIST      *Savage Winter*     $5.00

Orwig, Sara
  HM 71     *Camilla*           $4.00
  M&B       *Runaway Desire*    $20.00

Palmer, Diana
  Duets     (2 booksets/Silhouette)   $10.00/ea.
  MF 127    *Now and Forever*         $50.00
  MF 139    *Storm Over the Lady*     $50.00
  MF 150    *To Have and to Hold*     $50.00
  MF 179    *Sweet Enemy*             $50.00
  MF 218    *Love on Trial*           $50.00
  MF 223    *Dream's End*             $50.00

*Sara Orwig's*
Runaway Desire
*(Major Books, #3233).*
Courtesy of Jacque Tiegs.

**104**

| MF 250 | *Bound by a Promise* | $50.00 |
| MF | *If Winter Comes* | $50.00 |
| SD 12 | *Cowboy and the Lady, The* | $6.00 |
| SD 26 | *September Morning* | $5.00 |
| SD 50 | *Friends and Lovers* | $5.00 |
| SD 80 | *Fire and Ice* | $5.00 |
| SD 102 | *Snow Kisses* | $5.00 |
| SD 110 | *Diamond Girl* | $10.00 |
| SD 157 | *Rawhide Man* | $6.00 |
| SD 175 | *Lady Love* | $10.00 |
| SD 193 | *Cattleman's Choice* | $6.00 |
| SD 230 | *Tender Stranger, A* | $10.00 |
| SD 252 | *Love by Proxy* | $5.00 |
| SD 271 | *Eye of the Tiger* | $6.00 |
| SD 289 | *Loveplay* | $5.00 |
| SD 306 | *Rawhide and Lace* | $6.00 |
| SD 325 | *Rage of Passion* | $5.00 |
| SD 349 | *Fit for a King* | $5.00 |
| SD 391 | *Betrayed by Love* | $5.00 |
| SD 420 | *Enamored* | $6.00 |
| SD 469 | *Reluctant Father* | $5.00 |
| SD 492 | *Hoodwinked* | $4.00 |
| SR 254 | *Darling Enemy* | $6.00 |
| SR 301 | *Roomful of Roses* | $10.00 |
| SR 314 | *Heart of Ice* | $5.00 |
| SR 328 | *Passion Flower* | $5.00 |

*Group of novels by Diana Palmer: Long, Tall Texans titles for Silhouette including* Tyler *(#604),* Calhoun *(#580) and* Justin *(#592).*
Courtesy of Jacque Tiegs.

| SR 340 | *Soldier of Fortune (orig.)* | $25.00 |
| SR 406 | *After the Music* | $5.00 |
| SR 436 | *Champagne Girl* | $6.00 |
| SR 472 | *Unlikely Lover* | $5.00 |
| SR 532 | *Woman Hater* | $5.00 |
| SR 580 | *Calhoun* | $6.00 |
| SR 592 | *Justin* | $10.00 |
| SR 604 | *Tyler* | $6.00 |
| SR 670 | *Sutton's Way* | $6.00 |
| SR 694 | *Ethan* | $5.00 |
| SR 741 | *Connal* | $5.00 |
| SR 783 | *Harden* | $5.00 |
| SR 843 | *Donavan* | $5.00 |
| SSE 33 | *Heather's Song* | $4.00 |
| SSE 239 | *Australian, The* | $8.00 |

**Preston, Fayrene**

| LS 4 | *Silver Miracles* | $4.00 |
| LS 169 | *Burke, The Kingpin* | $6.00 |
| LSS | *Untamed Years, I, The* | $4.00 |
| LSS | *Untamed Years, II, The* | $4.00 |
| LS | *Sydney, The Temptress* | $6.00 |
| LS | *Silken Thunder* | $5.00 |
| LS | *Copper Fires* | $5.00 |

**Reno, Dawn**

| CONT | *All That Glitters* | $5.00 |

**Robbins, Kay**

| SD 73 | *Return Engagement* | $5.00 |
| SC 110 | *Taken by Storm* | $5.00 |
| SC 130 | *Elusive Dawn* | $5.00 |
| SC 190 | *Moonlight Rhapsody* | $5.00 |
| SC 262 | *Eye of the Beholder* | $5.00 |
| SD 322 | *Belonging to Taylor* | $5.00 |
| SD 378 | *On Her Doorstep* | $5.00 |

**Roberts, Nora**

| HH 4 | *Rebellion* | $4.00 |
| HH 21 | *Lawless* | $4.00 |
| HI 19 | *Night Moves* | $6.00 |
| CONT | *Sweet Revenge* | $4.00 |
| CONT | *Promise Me Tomorrow* | $10.00 |

*Nora Roberts' The O'Hurley's series: Photo of back cover shows the author on the left.* Skin Deep *(Silhouette Special Edition, #475). From the collection of Peg Reno.*

| CONT | *Sacred Sins* | $5.00 |
|---|---|---|
| CONT | *Hot Ice* | $5.00 |
| CONT | *Brazen Virtue* | $3.00 |
| SD 649 | *Man for Amanda, A* | $4.00 |
| SE 361 | *For Now, Forever* | $8.00 |
| SE 427 | *Local Hero* | $5.00 |
| SE 451 | *Last Honest Woman, The* | $6.00 |
| SE 463 | *Dance to the Piper* | $6.00 |
| SE 475 | *Skin Deep* | $6.00 |
| SE 499 | *Loving Jack* | $5.00 |
| SE 511 | *Best Laid Plans* | $6.00 |
| SE 553 | *Welcoming, The* | $3.00 |
| SE 625 | *Without a Trace* | $6.00 |
| SE 685 | *For the Love of Lilah* | $4.00 |
| SE 768 | *Captivated* | $4.00 |
| SE 774 | *Entranced* | $4.00 |
| SE 780 | *Charmed* | $4.00 |
| SIM 2 | *Once More with Feeling* | $3.00 |
| SIM 12 | *Tonight and Always* | $5.00 |
| SIM 25 | *This Magic Moment* | $6.00 |
| SIM 33 | *Endings and Beginnings* | $5.00 |
| SIM 40 | *Matter of Choice, A* | $5.00 |
| SIM 70 | *Rules of the Game* | $5.00 |
| SIM 85 | *Right Path, The* | $6.00 |
| SIM 94 | *Partners* | $5.00 |
| SIM 114 | *Boundary Lines* | $5.00 |
| SIM 123 | *Dual Image* | $6.00 |
| SIM 131 | *Art of Deception* | $6.00 |

*Nora Roberts's Language of Love set:* Her Mother's Keeper *(Silhouette, #20) and* Treasures Lost, Treasures Found *(Silhouette, #40). From the collection of Peg Reno.*

| | | |
|---|---|---|
| SIM 142 | *Affaire Royale* | $12.00 |
| SIM 150 | *Treasures Lost, Treasures Found* | $4.00 |
| SIM 160 | *Risky Business* | $6.00 |
| SIM 185 | *Mind Over Matter* | $6.00 |
| SIM 198 | *Command Performance* | $8.00 |
| SIM 212 | *Playboy Prince* | $8.00 |
| SIM 232 | *Irish Rose* | $4.00 |
| SIM 264 | *Name of the Game, The* | $4.00 |
| SIM 300 | *Gabriel's Angel* | $4.00 |
| SR 81 | *Irish Thoroughbred* | $4.00 |
| SR 127 | *Blithe Image* | $4.00 |
| SR 143 | *Song of the West* | $4.00 |
| SR 163 | *Search for Love* | $4.00 |
| SR 180 | *Island of Flowers* | $4.00 |
| SR 199 | *From This Day* | $4.00 |
| SR 215 | *Her Mother's Keeper* | $4.00 |
| SR 252 | *Untamed* | $4.00 |
| SR 274 | *Storm Warning* | $4.00 |
| SR 280 | *Sullivan's Woman* | $4.00 |
| SR 299 | *Less of a Stranger* | $4.00 |
| SR 529 | *Temptation* | $4.00 |
| SR 801 | *Courting Catherine* | $4.00 |
| SSE 59 | *Heart's Victory, The* | $4.00 |
| SSE 100 | *Reflections* | $4.00 |
| SSE 116 | *Dance of Dreams* | $4.00 |

*Two books in Nora Roberts's "MacGregor" series: Book One,* Playing the Odds *(Silhouette Special Edition) and Book Five,* For Now, Forever *(Silhouette Special Edition).* Courtesy of Jacque Tiegs.

| | | |
|---|---|---|
| SSE 162 | *First Impressions* | $4.00 |
| SSE 175 | *Law is a Lady, The* | $5.00 |
| SSE 199 | *Opposites Attract* | $4.00 |
| SSE 225 | *Playing the Odds* | $4.00 |
| SSE 235 | *Tempting Fate* | $4.00 |
| SSE 247 | *All the Possibilities* | $4.00 |
| SSE 259 | *One Man's Art* | $5.00 |
| SSE 271 | *Summer Desserts* | $4.00 |
| SSE 288 | *Second Nature* | $4.00 |
| SSE 306 | *One Summer* | $4.00 |
| SSE 318 | *Lessons Learned* | $4.00 |
| SSE 345 | *Will and a Way, A* | $5.00 |
| SSE 475 | *Skin Deep* | $4.00 |

Ryan, Nan

| | | |
|---|---|---|
| SD 351 | *Love in the Air* | $4.00 |
| HIST | *Midnight Affair* | $5.00 |
| HIST | *Outlaw's Kiss* | $10.00 |
| HIST | *Stardust* | $10.00 |

Ryan, Rachel

| | | |
|---|---|---|
| CE 21 | *Love's Encore* | $10.00 |
| CE 29 | *Love Beyond Reason* | $10.00 |
| CE 49 | *Eloquent Silence* | $10.00 |
| CE 59 | *Treasure Worth Seeking, A* | $10.00 |

St. Claire, Erin

| | | |
|---|---|---|
| SD 7 | *Not Even for Love* | $8.00 |

| SD 41 | *Seduction by Design* | $8.00 |
| SD 73 | *Kiss Remembered, A* | $8.00 |
| SD 139 | *Words of Silk* | $8.00 |
| SD 488 | *Thrill of Victory, A* | $5.00 |
| SIM 29 | *Secret Splendor, A* | $8.00 |
| SIM 76 | *Bittersweet Rain* | $8.00 |
| SIM 93 | *Sweet Anger* | $8.00 |
| SIM 112 | *Tiger Prince* | $8.00 |
| SIM 120 | *Led Astray* | $8.00 |
| SIM 133 | *Above and Beyond* | $8.00 |
| SIM 144 | *Honor Bound* | $8.00 |
| SIM 180 | *Devil's Own, The* | $8.00 |
| SIM 213 | *Two Alone* | $8.00 |

St. George, Margaret

| HA 462 | *A Pirate and His Lady* | $4.00 |

Shaw, Linda

| GLN | *Innocent Deception* | $8.00 |
| HIST | *Songbird* | $10.00 |

Shiplett, June Lund

| TT | *Journey to Yesterday* | $3.00 |
| TT | *Return to Yesterday* | $3.00 |

Simon, Joann

| TT | *Beloved Captain* | $10.00 |
| TT | *Hold Fast to Love* | $6.00 |
| TT | *Love Once Again* | $6.00 |
| TT | *Love Once in Passing* | $6.00 |

Smith, Debra

| HIST | *Follow the Sun (3-book set)* | $6.00 |

Stewart, Mary

| HIST | *Arthurian Saga (4 books)* | $20.00 |

Stuart, Anne

| CAN 501 | *Cameron's Landing* | $25.00 |
| CAN 523 | *Demonwood* | $30.00 |
| CAN 557 | *Demon Count, The* | $30.00 |
| CAN | *Demon Count's Daughter, The* | $30.00 |
| CAN 649 | *Lord Satan's Bride* | $30.00 |
| HP 5 | *Banish Misfortune* | $5.00 |
| HI 9 | *Catspaw* | $10.00 |
| HI 103 | *Catspaw II* | $4.00 |

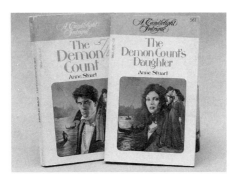

*Anne Stuart's* The Demon Count *and* The Demon Count's Daughter, *both Candlelight Intrigues. Courtesy of Jacque Tiegs.*

*Anne Stuart's* Banish Misfortune *(Harlequin American Romance Premier Edition, #5) and* Heart's Ease *(Harlequin American Romance, #39). Courtesy of Jacque Tiegs.*

*One of Anne Stuart's "Maggie Bennet" novels:* Darkness Before the Dawn *(Dell). Courtesy of Jacque Tiegs.*

*Jayne Taylor's*
Whirlwind Courtship
(*A Tiara Romance*).
Courtesy of Jacque Tiegs.

## Maggie Bennet Series

| | | |
|---|---|---|
| DELL/B | *Escape out of Darkness* | $25.00 |
| DELL/B | *Darkness Before the Dawn* | $25.00 |
| DELL/B | *At the Edge of the Sun* | $25.00 |
| GOTH | *Rose at Midnight, A* | $4.00 |
| GOTH | *Barrett's Hill* | $25.00 |
| GOTH | *Houseparty, The* | $15.00 |
| GOTH | *Seen and Not Heard* | $20.00 |
| DELL | *Maggie Bennet (3 books)* | $75.00 |

## Summers, Essie

| | | |
|---|---|---|
| HR | *Lake of the Kingfisher* | $2.00 |
| HR | *Adair of Starlight Peaks* | $2.00 |
| HR | *Return to Dragonshill* | $2.00 |
| HR | *Beyond the Foothills* | $2.00 |
| HR | *Anna of Strathallan* | $2.00 |
| HR 668 | *No Roses in June* | $5.00 |
| HR 724 | *House of the Shining Tide* | $5.00 |
| HR 775 | *Heatherleigh* | $5.00 |
| HR 785 | *Where No Roads Go* | $5.00 |
| HR 802 | *South to Forget* | $5.00 |
| HR 822 | *Time and the Place, The* | $5.00 |
| HR 847 | *Smoke and Fire, The* | $5.00 |
| HR 862 | *Moon Over the Alps* | $5.00 |
| HR 886 | *Bachelors Galore* | $5.00 |
| HR 910 | *Master of Tawhai, The* | $5.00 |
| HR 933 | *Bride in Flight* | $5.00 |
| HR 957 | *No Legacy for Lindsay* | $5.00 |
| HR 982 | *No Orchids by Request* | $5.00 |
| HR 1015 | *Sweet Are the Ways* | $5.00 |

*Rebecca York's*
Talons of the Falcon
(*The Peregrine Connection,*
*Dell*). *Courtesy of Jacque Tiegs.*

Taylor, Jayne

|  |  |  |
|---|---|---|
|  | *Whirlwind Courtship* | $10.00 |

Veryan, Patricia

| R | *Dedicated Villain, The* | $4.00 |
|---|---|---|
| R | *Give All to Love* | $4.00 |
| R | *Lord and The Gypsy* | $4.00 |
| R | *Love's Duet* | $4.00 |
| R | *Mistress of Willowvale* | $4.00 |
| R | *Wagered Widow, The* | $4.00 |
| R | *Practice to Deceive* | $4.00 |
| R | *Journey to Enchantment* | $4.00 |
| R | *Tyrant, The* | $4.00 |
| R | *Love Alters Not* | $4.00 |
| R | *Cherished Enemy* | $4.00 |
| R | *Feather Castles* | $4.00 |
| R | *Noblest Fraility, The* | $4.00 |
| R | *Nanette* | $4.00 |
| R | *Married Past Redemption* | $4.00 |
| R | *Sanguinet's Crown* | $4.00 |
| R | *Give All to Love* | $4.00 |
| R | *Some Brief Folly* | $10.00 |

Weir, Theresa

| F | *Amazon Lily* | $20.00 |
|---|---|---|

Winspear, Violet

| HR | *Beloved Castaway* | $2.00 |
|---|---|---|

York, Rebecca

| CONT | *Talons of the Falcon* | $20.00 |
|---|---|---|
| CONT | *In Search of the Dove* | 20.00 |

## INSTANT EXPERT QUIZ
(20 questions taken from the book)

1. What name did Diana Palmer use in the Silhouette Inspirationals line?

2. How did Sandra Brown get the name Rachel Ryan?

3. Name the author who wrote the teen romance for Wildfire, called *A Girl Named Summer*.

4. Name the three authors of the Shamrock Delaney saga.

5. What is the pseudonym of *New York Times* best selling author Barbara Delinsky?

6. Name all five of Jayne Ann Krentz's pseudonyms.

7. What is Kay Hooper's a.k.a. in the *Second Chance for Love* line?

8. What series did Karen A. Bale write?

9. What is Jude Deveraux's family name in her books?

10. What color is Nora Robert's book *Promise Me Tomorrow*?

11. Who wrote the Maggie Bennet series?

12. Who is the E. in A. E. Maxwell?

13. What is Joanne Redd's a.k.a.?

14. Who is Shannon Drake?

15. Whose picture is on the O'Hurleys books?

16. Who is the first author to pose with her husband on the cover of one of her historicals?

17. How many lines of books does Harlequin have?

18. How much is *Morci Battalion* worth?

19. How should paperback novels be stored?

20. Which two major romance lines joined to become the largest publisher of romances in the world?

# APPENDIX

## Glossary

**advance copy:** The copy of a book sent by publishers to writers for final approval; sometimes sent to reviewers before the publication date.

**anthology:** A collection of stories or novellas, usually centered around a theme.

**binding:** The part of the book where the title, author and publisher is printed so it is visible when the book is shelved; also called the "spine."

**blank leaves:** The empty pages at the beginning and end of most books.

**blurb:** A short quote on a book cover or in promotional material summarizing the book and/or its author.

**bodice-ripper:** A romance novel featuring the hero and heroine on the cover in a "clinch" pose, usually showing a great deal of chest and leg.

**bookmark:** The item used to hold one's place in a book.

**copy:** The wording on a book cover or in promotional material to advertise the book and its author.

**copyright page:** The page on the reverse of the title page where the date of the copyright/printing is listed.

**cover:** The front flap of a book to be used as promotional material, often sent to the author before the book is published.

**cover model:** The person used by the artist to illustrate the cover of a book (i.e. Fabio, Steve Sandalis, Tom Selleck, etc.)

**dog-eared:** Refers to the condition of a book's pages when they are bent at its corners.

**dust jacket:** The wrapper on a book which typically slips off a hardcover. The dust jacket often includes an author's photo and information, blurbs and some previous reviews for sales purposes.

**first edition:** The first time a book appears in printed form; this is usually the most collectible version of a book.

**futuristic:** A type of romance set in the future, in another world, place or time; often called science fiction; sometimes called time travel.

**galleys:** The final copy of the author's manuscript before it goes into print. This is what the publisher sends to the author for a final check.

**gothic:** The type of fiction set in Europe between the 12th and 16th century or a type of fiction that uses remote, gloomy and eerie settings to suggest mystery, horror and sinister dealings.

**manuscript:** The book in handwritten, typewritten or printed form before the book is bought and actually printed and bound.

**out of print:** The term used to denote a book which is no longer available from the publisher.

**press kit:** The materials used to promote a book. Usually includes a photo of the author, a copy of the book cover, a press release, copies of articles written about the author/book, and other pertinent information.

**print runs:** The number of books a publisher prints each time the book is put on the presses.

**Regency:** A romance set in Regency England (1811–20), the period during which George, Prince of Wales, acted as regent.

**remainder:** The unsold copies of a book the publisher then sells to a firm which specializes in selling "remainders."

**romantic suspense:** The type of romance in which the heroine is typically in trouble or suspects the hero of being something other than what he represents himself to be. Their romance is largely impeded by the suspenseful aspect of the story.

**science fiction:** Writing dealing with futuristic places and problems (often called futuristic, in the romance publishing world).

**search service:** The service a bookseller often provides to customers looking for out-of-print or hard-to-find books.

**time travel:** The type of romance in which the hero or heroine travels by some device to another time period where they find romance.

## *Bibliography*

Barnhart, Helene Schellenberg. *Writing Romance Fiction: For Love and Money*. Cincinnati: Writer's Digest Books, 1983.

Editors of the House of Collectibles. *The Official Price Guide to Old Books and Autographs, Seventh Edition*. New York: House of Collectibles/Random House, 1988.

Falk, Kathryn. *How to Write a Romance and Get It Published*. New York: Signet, 1984.

Lee, Linda. *How to Write and Sell Romance Novels: A Step-by-Step Guide*. Edmonds, Washington: Heartsong Press, 1988.

Lowery, Marilyn M. *How to Write Romance Novels That Sell*. New York: Rawson Associates, 1983.

Paludan, Eve. *The Romance Writer's Pink Pages: The Insider's Guide to Getting Your Romance Novel Published*. Rocklin, CA: Prima Publishing, 1994.

Sanders, George, Helen Sanders and Ralph Roberts. *The Price Guide to Autographs, Second Edition.* Randor, PA: Wallace-Homestead Book Company, 1991.

Editors of Twilight Publishing Group. *Essence of Romance.* Baton Rouge, LA: Twilight Publishing Group, Ltd., 1993.

Zeller, Leslie. *Book Collecting.* New York: Cornerstone Library, 1978.